HAMLYN
ALL COLOUR
INDOOR
GARDENING

HAMLYN
ALL COLOUR
INDOOR
GARDENING

HAMLYN

This book has been written by Suzy Powling and William Davidson
and compiled from material previously published by
Octopus Illustrated Publishing

Art Editor Liz Black Editor Anna Mumford
Picture Research Emily Hedges Production Michelle Thomas

Illustrations by Vicky Emptage
Symbols by Coryn Dickman

First published 1992
Hamlyn is an imprint of Octopus Illustrated Publishing,
part of Reed International Books Limited,
Michelin House, 81 Fulham Road, London SW3 6RB

A catalogue record for this book is available from
the British Library

ISBN 0 600 57447 4

Typeset in Sabon by Dorchester Typesetting Group Ltd, Dorchester

Produced by Mandarin Offset
Printed in Hong Kong

The Publishers would like to thank the following organizations and individuals
for their kind permission to reproduce the photographs in this book.

PICTURE ACKNOWLEDGEMENTS

The publishers would like to thank the following organisations and individuals for their kind permission to reproduce the photographs in this book:
Bernard Alfieri, 98 left; Heather Angel, 124 left; A-Z Botanical Collection, 74 left, 75 right; Peter Black, 113 right; Michael Boys Syndication, 17, 22 right; Pat Brindley, 20, 56 right, 61 left, 63 right, 81 right, 95, 103 right, 107 left and right; W. H. Brown, 120 left and right, 122 left and right, 123 left, 125 left and right, back cover bottom left; Camera Press/IMS, 8, 73; Bruce Coleman Ltd/Eric Crichton, 58 left; John Cowley, 83 left; Eric Crichton, 24 left, 32 right, 37 left and right, 39 left, 42 right, 43 left, 45, 49 left, 53 left, 54 right, 55 left, 59 right, 60 left, 62 left and right, 63 left, 69 right, 71 left, 77 right, 80 left, 81 left, 82 right, 83 right, 86 right, 87 left, 88 right, 89 right, 90 left, 91 right, 92 left and right, 93 left, 96 right, 97 right, 99 left, 100 right, 101 right, 102 right, 108 left and right, 109 left and right, 112 left and right, 114 left and right, 115 left and right, 117 left and right, front cover left, centre and right, back cover top centre and bottom right; W. F. Davidson, 23 right; Good Housekeeping/ Jan Baldwin, 18; Melvin Grey, 61 right; Guiseppe Mazza, 89 left, 98 right; Octopus Picture Library, 29 left, 48 right, 106 left, back cover top right; Octopus Publishing Group Ltd., /Theo Bergstrom, 25 right, /Michael Boys, 27 left, /W. F. Davidson, 35 left, 51 left, /Melvin Grey, 6, 64, 118, /Jerry Harpur, 60 right, /Neil Holmes, 31 left, 57 right, 85, /John Moss, 25 left, 97 left, /Roger Phillips, 29 right, 48 left, 50 left, 66 right, 106 right, /Peter Rauter, 28 left, 30 right, 31 right, 32 left, 34 left and right, 35 right, 40 left, 42 left, 47 right, 52 right, 54 left, /George Wright, 36 left, 56 left, back cover top left; Chris Page, 66 left, 67 left and right, 68 left, 69 left, 70 right, 76 left; Frances Perry, 96 left; Photos Horticultural/ Michael Warren, 52 left, 75 left, 79, 103 left; Harry Smith Collection, 22 left, 23 left, 26 left, 27 right, 28 right, 30 left, 33 left and right, 36 right, 38 left and right, 39 right, 40 right, 41 left and right, 43 right, 46 left and right, 47 left, 50 right, 51 right, 53 left and right, 57 left, 58 right, 59 left, 68 right, 70 left, 71 right, 74 right, 77 left, 80 right, 87 right, 88 left, 90 right, 91 left, 93 right, 99 right, 100 left, 101 left, 102 left, 104, 113 left, 116 left and right, 121 left; Spectrum Colour Library, 26 right; Peter Stiles, 24 right, 82 left, 86 left; Suttons Seeds, 49 right, 55 right; Ward Lock/ Bob Challinor from *Art of Indoor Bonsai* by John Ainsworth, 121 right, 123 right, 124 right; Elizabeth Whiting and Associates, 12, 72, 111, / G. Henderson, 76 right.

CONTENTS

INTRODUCTION

Every modern home boasts a number of indoor plants among its decorative features. No matter what your style, it is certain to be enhanced by a clever grouping of foliage plants or a flowering plant in brilliant display. So many beautiful plants are now available that it can be difficult to make a choice. To make the selection easier in the first instance, the plants described in this book are divided into 10 main groups: foliage plants; flowering plants; ferns; palms; bulbs; cacti; succulents; bromeliads; orchids, and bonsai. Each of these groups has different characteristics, and within the groups the species have individual needs. Every one is illustrated in colour to help you identify your choice. We appreciate indoor plants for their long-lasting appeal as much as for the refreshing note that living plants introduce to any room setting.

Success with house plants depends on selecting species that will thrive in the conditions you have to offer. Throughout this book, emphasis is placed on how to match the plant to the environment. Easy-to-use reference symbols are given to indicate the important factors of size, requirements for light and humidity and the minimum winter temperature that can be tolerated. Flowering time is given where relevant. Each entry describes the plant and its most interesting varieties, giving detailed information about keeping it healthy and raising new plants where this is feasible in the home.

A beautiful indoor display can be composed of plants that are easy to grow but perennially rewarding; keen gardeners can practise their skills on more demanding species; real enthusiasts can concentrate on exotics like orchids or bonsai that call for special care. Whether you are a keen amateur or a devoted enthusiast, you will find dozens of plants among the 170 and more described here to bring life and colour to your home.

PLANTS FOR INDOORS

Such is the diversity of plants for indoor cultivation that no home need be without the enlivening effect of foliage and flowers. For those who have no space outdoors, growing plants indoors provides an opportunity for frustrated gardeners to practise their creative talents. The joy of indoor gardening is that because the warmer environment of the home makes it possible to nurture species too tender for life outside, even those lucky enough to have conventional flowerbeds will be attracted by the idea of raising more exotic species such as bromeliads, orchids and cacti in the house. There is a houseplant for every situation and to suit every taste: the design element is as important when choosing plants for indoor settings as it is outside, though the criteria may be different. Most important is

choosing plants which will be happy and healthy in the environment you can provide.

No matter where they come from, all plants need light, warmth, water and nourishment to survive. In their natural habitat the plants which we cultivate indoors receive exactly what they need in order to thrive; indeed many of them reach very much greater dimensions in the South American jungle or the idyllic climate of South Africa than they do when confined to a pot. When grown indoors, however, it is the gardener's skill in imitating nature which determines how healthy any specimen will be. Every entry in this book includes a set of symbols which briefly summarize a plant's individual needs as far as light, humidity and minimum winter temperature is concerned, but it is

An interesting but restful effect is achieved by grouping together plants with different leaf shapes and habits.

useful to understand how these factors act and interact to maintain health. The first step to healthy indoor plants is choosing specimens which have been carefully grown and which are sold in peak condition. An obviously unhealthy plant will have yellowing leaves which may be drooping or suffering from drought; but some plants which look healthy enough may, once you get them home, go into a decline from which they never recover. This is most likely to happen in winter with foliage plants which are displayed outside the shop or on a market stall within a short time of leaving the automatically controlled atmosphere of a heated commercial greenhouse. If you want to buy houseplants in winter, buy them from shops which are kept warm and where they are stored away from draughts. Check that the compost is nicely moist. Choose tough plants like ivy, sansevieria or fatsia rather than the fussier kinds like codiaeum, maranta or tropical palms. Minimize their exposure to cold on the way home; keep them well wrapped and do not carry them around while you do more shopping. Put them in the car instead or take them home straight away. Repotting should not be necessary, but if you want to set a group of plants in a single container, wait for two or three weeks to let them become acclimatized to their new environment.

CHOOSING PLANTS

Plants admired for the beauty of their foliage look very tempting displayed in the shop or garden centre, but it can be disappointing to get your purchase home and discover too late that you cannot meet its particular needs. The chart on page 11 gives a guide to the plants which thrive in particular situations. Check before making your choice. Names in bold type need a humid atmosphere.

Hallways present particular problems for plants, especially if they are unheated, because of the inevitable draughts. Despite the unfavourable circumstances, fatshedera, fatsia, hedera and tolmeia will be happy enough as long as the light is good. Hedera and tolmeia can even cope with poor light (and if your hall is cold and dark, you will be glad of plants to cheer it up). Ideally, assess the kind of environment each room has to offer *before* going to the garden centre and choose plants to suit them.

CARE OF PLANTS

Looking at a garden through the seasons, it is easy to see that plants have a life cycle. The vast majority start into growth in spring, growing rapidly in the warmth and sunshine of summer, fading in autumn and resting and recuperating during the winter. Though the stages are not so clear, most indoor plants have a similar life cycle. The exceptions are those which are forced to flower in winter, or annuals which complete the cycle in one year and are then discarded. The resting period is important, allowing the plant time to build up its strength for the next season. Requirements for water and food diminish during dormancy. The amount and intensity of light is naturally less during the winter; this may suit the plant, or it may be necessary to reposition it to meet its needs.

Water More houseplants have met a premature end through an excess of water – or from drought – than any other causes. Plants like cyperus, which like to 'have their feet in water', are exceptional. Most will not survive if the compost is so waterlogged that air cannot get to the roots. If any water is left in the plant saucer 30 minutes after watering, tip it away. While giving to each plant according to its needs as described in the relevant entry, do not water without testing the compost first. Though it looks dry on the surface, it may be sufficiently moist beneath. Insert a small stick into the compost; if it comes out sticky, water is not needed. Clay pots make a dull sound when tapped if the compost is damp.

Different types of plants vary dramatically in their need for water, from cacti, fitted for life in the arid desert, to marsh plants like the acorus. The immediate environment also has an important effect. In hot, dry weather or in heated rooms, moisture evaporates from the potting mixture and much is lost through transpiration from the leaves. When it is cool, moisture is retained for much longer. Most important, plants need much more water during the period of active growth than when resting, when very little indeed may be enough – as always, depending on the individual.

To apply water, use a light watering can with a long, narrow spout so that you can aim the flow directly on to the potting mixture without wetting leaves or flowers. Some plants, such as cyclamen, must be watered

TOOLS AND EQUIPMENT

Pots, pot saucers and composts are obvious essentials. Keep two mist-sprays, one for water and one for insecticides/fungicides. A watering can is much the best way to apply water.

1. Clay pots (various sizes)
2. Clay half pots
3. Plastic pots (various sizes)
4. Plant saucers
5. Bags of soil-based, peat-based and seed composts.
6. Two mist-sprays
7. Watering can with thin spout
8. Liquid fertilizer
9. Small natural sponges
10. Mini-trowel and fork
11. Bamboo canes
12. Fine stakes
13. Trellis frame
14. Moss-covered stake (in pot)
15. Secateurs
16. Twine
17. Plant ties (metal rings)
18. Hygrometer
19. Maximum-minimum thermometer
20. Seed trays and pans.

from below as the tuber should never get wet. Others may be so bushy that the surface of the compost is inaccessible. In these cases place water in the saucer. The plant will take up what it needs within 30 minutes. After this period, empty the saucer.

Remember that a large pot will dry out more quickly than a small one as a greater surface area is exposed to the air; evaporation is faster from an unglazed clay pot than a glazed or plastic one, and growing mixtures containing sand, grit or perlite encourage fast drainage.

To revive a parched plant, first carefully break up the surface of the compost with a small fork, without damaging the roots. Plunge the pot in a bucket of water, holding it until bubbles stop rising. Spray the leaves with a fine mist at the same time. Let the excess water drain away and replace the plant in a suitable position. If the problem soon recurs, try repotting with fresh mixture.

Humidity Water vapour present in the air – the humidity level – is not related to how moist the potting mixture is. Nor is it easy to judge: the only time you can *see* water vapour is in mist or fog. Nevertheless, it can be measured by an instrument called a hygrometer, and many indoor gardeners use one (in conjunction with a thermometer) to ensure that humidity levels are correct. A reading of about 60 per cent suits most plants, but generally speaking those with thin, papery leaves like fittonias need more. All plants need increased humidity in higher temperatures. The simplest way to provide this is to stand the pot in a shallow tray holding a layer of pebbles at least 5cm/2in deep (up to 15cm/6in for very large pots). Pour in water without letting the water level rise higher than the pebbles (otherwise it may be absorbed by the potting mixture), and keep them moist. It is a good idea to group plants that need high humidity together, as they trap water vapour between the leaves and benefit each other. Hanging baskets often have built-in drip trays which can be used to hold water *below* the pot, so that water vapour rises around the leaves. It also helps to stand the pot containing the plant in another, larger pot containing peat kept constantly damp.

Feeding Regular feeding with a liquid fertilizer can make a tremendous difference to the health of houseplants. Most need feeding during the active period of growth (usually spring and summer), with little or none in the dormant period. Allowing unused nutrients to remain in the compost can lead to an accumulation of harmful salts. If you have been regularly feeding a plant which has not put on much growth, flush the pot out with water at the next two waterings and do not resume feeding until the plant shows signs of growth. After repotting, it is best not to feed for two or three months as the roots could be damaged.

Liquid fertilizers are useful as you can feed and water your plants at the same time. Top dressings are also available, which are sprinkled on to the surface of the compost. Sticks and tablets which are pushed into the compost last between four and eight weeks. As a plant can only make use of nutrients if they are dissolved in water, you must remember to water them regularly.

How much growth plants make depends directly on how much light they get. A pelargonium on a sunny windowsill might well appreciate a weekly feed, but if sited away from the window a feed every two weeks would be enough. Cacti, succulents, bromeliads, ferns and some palms need less feeding than the majority of plants. Having said that, plants in large pots need more feeding, and mature palms may well be in large pots.

Do not feed a plant just because it looks poorly; it may be in the wrong potting mixture, in the wrong situation, waterlogged or parched, so check these points first. And do not exceed the recommended dose: an overconcentration of fertilizers may well damage the roots. Foliar feeds made up to the correct strength and sprayed on to the leaves are useful as a quick pick-me-up when routine feeding has been neglected.

Temperature While it is true that all plants need a certain degree of warmth, the relationship between temperature and the amount of available light, water and humidity cannot be overemphasized. In higher temperatures, increased amounts of water and lighting levels are essential. The minimum temperature which individual plants tolerate is variable. In winter, poor light means slow or zero growth, for which low temperatures are needed (and, in nature, given). This is the important rest period in which many plants build up their strength for the summer. Tender plants which cannot tolerate temperatures lower than 16°C/61°F need correspondingly moderate, not poor, light at this time.

Constancy of temperature at all times of year is important: while a drop of several degrees at night is natural, dramatic fluctuations during the day are harmful. This is why plants should not be positioned in a draught, and why windowsills are not always the best place. Intense heat can be generated through glass, which quickly changes to relative chill when the window is opened.

Many houseplants are of tropical origin and thrive in hot summers, but those from temperate zones such as fatshedera will not be happy. They need a cool and airy position, as do many flowering plants.

Light Plants such as cacti can tolerate many hours of direct sunlight. Palms need bright but filtered light, with only a few hours of direct sunlight every day. In nature, ferns are sheltered from direct sunlight by the foliage of the trees under which they grow. Flower production depends on adequate bright light. Different plants obviously have varying needs, and the wise indoor gardener will identify them. Meeting them will be easier with some understanding of the effects of direct light. For example, an unobstructed sunny

TEMPERATURE CHECK CHART

	Suitable temperature range		
	18–24°C/ 64–75°F	13–18°C/ 55–64°F	7–13°C/ 45–55°F
BRIGHT, INDIRECT LIGHT			
Adiantum	x		
Aphelandra	x		
Asplenium	x	x	
Begonia rex	x		
Caladium	x		
Calathea	x		
Chamaedorea		x	x
Chlorophytum		x	x
Cissus	x	x	
Cocos		x	x
Codiaeum	x		
Cyperus	x	x	x
Dracaena	x	x	
Dizygotheca	x		
Ficus benjamina			
Ficus elastica		x	x
Ficus pumila			
Hedera		x	x
Howea		x	
Hypoestes		x	
Maranta			
Nephrolepis	x	x	
Pellaea		x	
Peperomia		x	
Philodendron	x	x	
Pilea	x	x	
Pteris	x	x	
Sansevieria	x	x	x
Scindapsus	x	x	
Tolmeia			x
Tradescantia		x	x
Yucca		x	x
POOR LIGHT			
Adiantum	x		
Cissus	x	x	
Cyperus	x	x	x
Hedera		x	x
Maranta	x		
Nephrolepis	x	x	
Philodendron	x	x	
Scindapsus	x	x	
Tolmeia			x
SUNNY POSITION			
Cacti	x		
Cyperus	x	x	x
Hedera		x	x
Hypoestes		x	
Peperomia		x	
Pilea	x	x	
Sansevieria	x	x	x
Succulents			x
Tolmeia			x
Tradescantia		x	x
Yucca		x	x

This pretty bamboo plant gently brings some outdoor qualities indoors to great effect.

window will admit direct sunlight for most of the day. It can be filtered, if necessary, by a fine blind or curtain, or if there is a leafy tree outside. The light at a short distance from the window will still be bright. At a distance of about 2.4m/8ft the light could be called moderate. The areas to the side of even a brightly lit window receive much less light than you might think.

Poor light in dark corners or by obstructed windows is insufficient for most plants. One solution is artificial lighting. Ordinary light bulbs will not do, as they generate too much heat and scorch the leaves. They may be used at reasonable distances to emphasize an arrangement for decorative purposes, but have no practical value. Suitable artificial lighting systems include mercury blended lamps, which are rather expensive to run, but the best choice is fluorescent tubes, available in a wide range of shapes and sizes.

Versions of high pressure mercury lamps and metal halide lamps, widely used by commercial growers, are available from specialist outlets.

It is advisable to place plants against a white or light background, where a certain amount of available light will be reflected back on to them. Plants next to dark walls will grow towards a source of light much more markedly than those next to pale walls, giving a lop-sided appearance. To help even growth, give plants a quarter turn every two weeks or so. Do not turn a flowering plant that is already in bud as the sudden change in light levels may cause the buds to drop off. Stiff-leaved species and rosette-forming kinds do not turn to the light in this way.

Plant hygiene Plants not only look better when kept clean, but are likely to be healthier. Sponging with tepid water removes mites, insects and their eggs along with the dust which prevents light getting to the foliage. Palm fronds can be cleansed more easily by standing the plant outside in a gentle summer shower.

Support systems Climbing plants, which if left to themselves would become a messy, unhealthy jumble of stems, need to be trained up bamboo canes, trellis-work frames or a moss-covered stake. Whatever system is appropriate, it should be as inconspicuous as possible. If necessary, tie young growths in loosely using twine or fine metal rings. Put the stakes in position when repotting, taking care not to damage the roots. The moss on stakes for philodendrons and other plants with aerial roots must always be moist. Test with the fingertips and mist-spray when necessary.

Holiday care You cannot expect your houseplants to survive two or more weeks' neglect without suffering to some extent. Ask a friend or neighbour to take care of them while you are away, making the task easier if possible by grouping the plants together and leaving watering can and liquid feed ready to hand. If no such help is forthcoming, a few simple strategies will stave off disaster. Move plants out of direct sunlight. To conserve moisture, first remove all flowers and flower-buds, if any. Water the plants well and cover each one with a polythene bag. Blow it up first so that it will not touch the leaves and keep it in place with a rubber band. Alternatively, put all the pots in boxes, packed round with moist peat. Another simple watering system works by capillary action. Fill a bucket with water and position the potted plants around it. Tie a weight to one end of a 2.5cm/1in lamp wick (you will need one for each plant) and drop it in the water. Insert the other end of the wick into the compost of a pot. It is as well to try this system out for a week or so *before* going away to make sure water is getting to the plants and not on your furniture. For prize specimens it may be worth investing in self-watering pots. These contain a reservoir of water in the base which will usually keep the plants going for up to four weeks.

Pruning 'Pruning' conjures up images of wrestling with tangled rose bushes rather than any task associated with potted plants. But houseplants do need cutting to shape sometimes, or even cutting down to

WHAT CAN GO WRONG?

Pests and diseases afflict many plants but most problems that arise are caused by over- or underwatering, too low humidity, poor light and other cultural deficiencies, as described below. If the symptoms are not too far developed, plants generally recover when ideal conditions are restored.

SYMPTOMS	CAUSE
Lower leaves limp and yellowing. Flower drop. Soggy soil.	Overwatering
Leaves and stem wilting. Brown leaf tips. New leaves fail to develop.	Underwatering
Brown leaf edges, leaf drop.	Dry atmosphere
Lower leaves dry up, flowers fade quickly.	Overheating
Previously healthy plant drops leaves, which turn yellow.	Sudden change in environment
Long spindly stems reaching for light. New leaves too small. Variegated plants lose colouring.	Poor light
Leaves spotted brown, turning crisp.	Light too bright
Fast but feeble growth, white deposit on surface of compost.	Overfeeding
Failure to grow. Poor leaf colour. New leaves too small.	Underfeeding
Roots bulging through drainage holes and rising at surface of compost. Poor growth.	Needs repotting

size. The most frequently employed form of pruning is pinching out, that is removing the small growing point of a stem in order to produce bushy growth. It is important for tradescantias, coleus and beloperone, for example, which would otherwise become spindly. Pinching out can often be done with finger and thumb, but on tougher stems sharp scissors are more effective.

Cutting back is the term used when the main stem or a mature sideshoot (rather than the growing tip) has to be shortened to keep the plant size in reasonable bounds, as in reducing a ceiling-height *Ficus elastica* (rubber plant). Use pruning secateurs to make a clean cut, straight across the stem, as close to a growth bud as possible. Cutting back the main stem encourages sideshoots and vice versa.

Potting mixtures A number of reliable composts are commercially available, made up in different formulas to meet the needs of different plants at different stages of development. While exotic plants like orchids have very particular requirements, most are reasonably easy-going. This is not to say they would be happy in a potful of garden soil of questionable quality and probably carrying weed seeds, pests and diseases.

Soil-based mixtures are relatively heavy, an advantage for top-heavy plants, and they contain certain nutrients. Peat-based mixtures are light and easy to work with but are quite lacking in nutrients, so regular plant feeding is essential. When raising plants from seed, always start off with a good quality proprietary seed compost.

To top-dress a plant which is in the largest pot size you have room for, scrape away the top layer of old compost with a small trowel, taking care not to damage the roots or to expose too many of them. Fill up the pot with fresh compost to which some slow-release fertilizer has been added. Add enough compost to reach the previous level. Top-dressing should be done at the time when repotting would normally be carried out.

When potting on, prepare a pot or other container by placing crocks and moist compost on the base. Ensure that the compost of the plant to be moved is moist all the way through. Remove the plant from its existing pot by pulling the fingers of one hand across the compost surface, turning it upside down with the other hand and gently tapping the rim on a work surface. The plant will slide out. Cut back any long roots, place in the new container and fill compost around the sides firming with your fingers.

PROPAGATION

While some houseplants can only be successfully raised from seed in specialist nurseries, a number can easily be grown at home by various methods. Raising your own plants is one of the most creative aspects of gardening, indoors or out, and can save money too. The most common forms of propagation are described below.

SOWING SEED

Browallias, cinerarias, exacums, impatiens, pelargoniums and primulas can be raised from seed. Most are sown in early spring, but variations are given in individual entries.

Fill a seed tray with most seed compost and press it down evenly and firmly. Place the seeds on top, evenly spaced. Cover with 5mm/$\frac{1}{4}$in of sifted compost (unless the seeds are very fine) and water in gently until the compost is thoroughly wet (Fig 1a). Cover with a sheet of glass or polythene and place in a heated frame or propagator; or cover with a plastic bag and place in a warm place away from light, such as an airing cupboard (Fig 1b). Check daily for moisture on the inside of the bag, and flick it off. As soon as the seed leaves appear, remove the cover and move to a protected position in the light. When the true leaves appear the seedlings can be pricked off into trays or 7.5cm/3in pots of potting compost (Fig 1c). Prepare planting holes with a pencil, spacing them 4cm/$1\frac{1}{2}$ in apart. Carefully remove a small clump of seedlings with a plastic plant tag or similar tool, holding them by the leaves, never the roots. Separate them gently and lower them one by one into the planting holes. Use a pencil to firm the compost around each one. Water in using a fine rose watering can. Place the tray in a cold frame or on a windowsill away from direct sunlight for two or three days, then move into a sunlit position. Keep the compost moist. Gradually expose the seedlings to the environment they will occupy as mature plants. Transfer to pots of the standard growing mixture when well established.

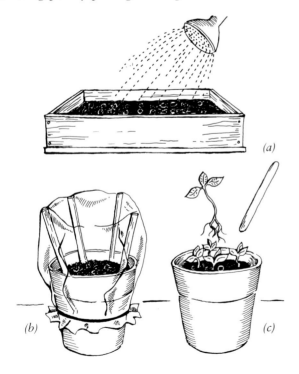

Fig 1 Sowing seed and pricking out.

Tip cuttings Many plants can be increased by tip cuttings, notably impatiens, tradescantia and zebrina, which have hollow stems, as well as all the ivies (hedera species).

Using a sharp blade, take 7.5cm/3in cuttings (or as given in individual entries) at the recommended time (Fig 2a). Remove the lower leaves and trim the stem just below a leaf node (Fig 2b). Stand the cutting in a small container of water (Fig 2c). When roots have appeared, about two weeks later, pot up the cutting in standard compost.

For plants without hollow stems, root the cuttings directly in small pots containing a mixture of peat and sand in equal quantities, or a proprietary potting compost. Make 4-6 holes around the edge of the pot with a small dibber or pencil. Insert each cutting so that the stem is supported by the edge of the pot (Fig 2d). Soak the compost with water and let the excess drain away (Fig 2e). Enclose the pot in a polythene bag, blown up so that it does not touch the leaves, and secure with a rubber band (Fig 2f). Leave in the shade at a steady 18°C/64°F. Keep the compost moist. The tips will show new growth when the cuttings have rooted, about four weeks later. Separate the cuttings carefully and pot them up individually in the standard compost. Gradually acclimatize them to the conditions recommended for mature plants.

Leaf cuttings To increase your stock of saintpaulias, sinningias and other fleshy-leaved plants, take leaf cuttings in summer.

Remove two or three healthy leaves, each with about 5cm/2in length of stalk, and trim the end with a sharp knife. Insert in evenly spaced holes made in small pots containing peat and sand in equal quantities or a proprietary potting compost. The stalks should fit neatly in the holes when gently firmed in, but the leaves must stand clear of the compost. Treat as tip cuttings, watching out for any excess condensation on the inside of the polythene bag. The appearance of tiny new leaves within four or five weeks indicates that rooting has occurred. Separate the cuttings carefully and pot them up individually in the standard compost. Keep warm and shaded for a further four weeks before treating as mature plants.

Numerous new *Begonia rex* plants can be raised from a single leaf by a fascinating method. In summer, select a large healthy leaf and cut it cleanly from the parent plant (Fig 3a). Trim the stem to 1cm/½in. Make

Fig 2 Tip cuttings.

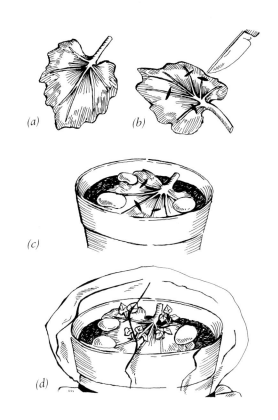

Fig 3 Leaf cuttings.

small cuts on the underside of the leaf where the main veins meet (Fig 3b). Place the whole leaf cut side down on a seed tray containing moistened potting compost, and anchor it with a few pieces of broken clay pot or clean pebbles (Fig 3c). Cover with polythene and keep at 21°C/70°F. Tiny plantlets will arise from the cuts within four to five weeks (Fig 3d). Remove the polythene and keep warm and shaded for a further two or three weeks before potting up in 7.5cm/3in pots.

It is also easy to increase sansevierias from leaf cuttings. Take a single leaf from a mature plant, cutting it away at the base with a sharp blade. Cut the leaf into horizontal sections, each about 2.5cm/1in deep. Place the sections four to a 12.5cm/5in pot of moist potting compost, making sure the lower end is set downwards. Give them a mist-spray and cover the pot with a polythene bag secured with a rubber band. Keep shaded at 21°C/70°F. New leaves will emerge from the base of each section within six to eight weeks. Remove the polythene and pot up in 7.5cm/3in pots.

Offsets Many different types of plants produce offsets or suckers at the base. Once these infants have achieved about half the height of the parent plant they can be detached and potted up individually. Summer is the best time to do this. Remove the whole plant from its pot, carefully shake off the soil from the root ball and separate out the rooted offset(s). If the parent plant is exhausted you may decide to discard it, or it may be well worth repotting. Fill small pots with compost to the three-quarter mark. Insert a thin bamboo stake if the offset is likely to need support. To pot up a single offset, hold it in the pot with the crown 1cm/2in below the rim, and with your other hand trickle compost around it until the pot is full; firm it down and water well, letting the excess drain away.

Division Splitting a mature plant into sections is an easy method of propagation used for chlorophytum, aspidistra, fittonia, sansevieria and adiantum, plants which all have numerous stems arising from beneath the surface of the compost. It can be done at any time during the period of active growth. Remove the plant from its pot and use your fingers to ease away the compost so that you can see the best places to divide the roots. It is usually possible to tear them apart, but occasionally a sharp knife is needed if the roots are

tough. Repot each section immediately in the standard compost, firming them in well. Water sparingly and keep warm and shaded until well established.

AIR LAYERING

This specialized method of propagation, appropriate to *Ficus benjamina* (weeping fig) and *F. elastica* (rubber plant) as well as dizygotheca, will appeal to the more experienced gardener. It should be done in spring. Make a length of stem bare of leaves by removing those within 23cm/9in of the topmost cluster (Fig 4a). Cut them off cleanly, flush with the stem. Make a slanting upward cut 5cm/2in long just below a leaf node (Fig 4b). Ease it open and brush with hormone rooting powder. Place a polythene tube around the cut, attaching it securely to the stem with tape. Fill the bag with moistened sphagnum moss (Fig 4c and d). Close the bag at the top with more tape. Roots should issue from the cut within ten weeks. Detach the rooted plant by cutting it from the parent just below the bag (the old plant will produce sideshoots and can be kept if it still looks good). Pot up in the standard compost and keep warm, shaded and just moist until well established (Fig 4e).

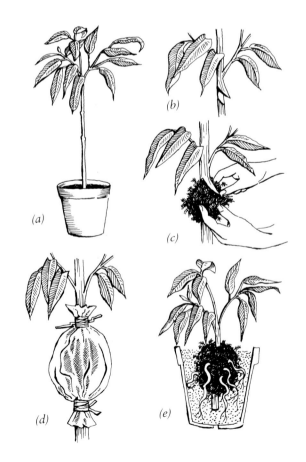

Fig 4 Air layering Ficus benjamina, F. elastica *and dizygotheca.*

A pair of healthy yuccas flanking a doorway add a mediterranean feel to an interior.

DESIGNING WITH HOUSEPLANTS

Every room in the house can be enhanced by plants, though some are better suited to certain situations. While the entrance hall is a place which should be welcoming it is often distinctly inhospitable for plants. A well-lit, airy hall offers scope for flowering plants that prefer cooler temperatures, such as cineraria and calceolaria. A bowl of spring bulbs would add colour – and scent too, if you include hyacinths. Space is likely to be limited, so avoid spreading or trailing foliage that may be damaged. A pedestal may provide the answer, supporting a decorative container with an arching fern or aspidistra. A stairwell lit from above by a skylight can be filled with hanging baskets or a shelf of trailing plants such as hedera, tradescantia or *Ficus pumila*. On the staircase itself, if space permits, the climber *Philodendron scandens* can be sited to great effect. As the amount and direction of light in most halls is problematic, it may well be worth installing an artificial lighting system to increase the range of possibilities.

In the kitchen Kitchens are popular spots for indoor plants; in a traditional, country-style room they fit per-

fectly with the warmth of wooden surfaces on which collections of favourite china sit beside bowls of fruit and piles of cookery books. In modern, clinical kitchens, plants are the perfect way to soften hard angles and straight lines, to offset the glint of chrome and glass with harmonious greens in arching forms. The problem with many kitchens is the likely fluctuation in temperature. In basically functional rooms, play safe with chlorophytum, tradescantia, chamaedorea and the tougher ferns. In rooms used by a family all day – and therefore kept steadily warm – add an asplenium, some pileas and peperomia. Gas fumes can only be tolerated by an aspidistra, and even that will need ventilation. Situate plants where they will not be disturbed. Hanging baskets are ideal, leaving surfaces clear, and shelves are suitable, as long as you can reach them easily enough to care for the plants. A small sunny window fitted with glass shelves is the ideal home for a group of succulents, their distinctive shapes outlined against the light.

In the bathroom Temperature and humidity levels fluctuate more dramatically in the bathroom than any other room. This limits the choice of plants that will do well – the warmth and humidity created by a steamy bath is great for exotics as long as it lasts, but for the rest of the time the room may be rather chilly, as windows are opened to release the steam. Ivies (hedera species) do well in colder rooms, but if a heated towel rail or small radiator keeps the temperature at a higher level, include philodendron and try a calathea. An all-white bathroom with mirrors and natural light will be good news for plants, and in aesthetic terms the perfect setting for fresh green ferns cascading over the sides of their containers. The leaves of all plants will need frequent cleaning if talcum powder and aerosol sprays are used. Plants may need an occasional break from the bathroom: move them to a steadier environment for a while.

In the bedroom People rarely choose to make a display of houseplants in the bedroom, but it is probably the room best suited to this purpose. The temperature is steady, and likely to be on the cool side, with correspondingly healthy levels of humidity. Perhaps setting out a fine display of foliage and flowering plants in the bedroom will encourage you to spend more time in it.

If the light is good, a yucca will do well, as will the reliable aspidistra. *Cissus antartica* needs a little more warmth, hederas will thrive, and many flowering plants do very well. Complement a blue colour scheme with streptocarpus, hydrangea or campanula. Add bright pink with cyclamen and azalea; if there is a sunny window, introduce pelargoniums. In winter, the bedroom is an excellent home for resting plants.

In the living room The design of the living room inevitably merits a good deal of attention as the busiest room in the house and the most likely to be seen by visitors. The contribution made by foliage and flowers can and should be much greater than the odd potted plant on a side table. Houseplants can completely change a room's ambience, becoming a permanent feature in the overall design in a way that bunches of cut flowers cannot do. Some might choose bold, eyecatching plants like *Ficus elastica* or a large-leaved philodendron, a yucca or magnificent palm. Exotic bromeliads are at home in modern settings, and are always a talking point. Ferns are the most versatile plants, their delicacy and grace inviting a sense of peace and blending with light, spare rooms as well as

cosy, homely interiors. They bring a note of calm to colourful, busy rooms, as do *Ficus benjamina*, cyperus, cissus and the elegant spathiphyllum. Low-growing plants such as fittonia, saintpaulia, *Ficus pumila*, tolmeia, schlumbergera and the pileas are beautiful viewed from above if set on a low table. Groups of plants playing on a variety of leaf shape and colour, some bushy, some upright and with different heights look stunning, and are the best way of adding interest to dull (not dark) corners. Plants with similar needs can be set in a single pot; another way to unify different species is to place all in similar containers – a row of identical pots, whether shining white or decorated in Mediterranean colours, looks disciplined but pleasing to the eye.

The constraints of light, temperature and humidity apply here as elsewhere in the house: advantages are that living rooms are generally kept reasonably and steadily warm and free of draughts. An atmosphere polluted by cigarette smoke is as unhealthy for plants as it is for humans – if this is a problem ensure adequate ventilation or move plants to a cleaner environment for a while.

In mid-winter bowlfuls of cyclamen add a cheering note of colour.

PESTS AND DISEASES

PEST	SYMPTOMS	REMEDY
Aphids (greenfly)	Suck the sap from leaves and stems, which become discoloured, distorted and stunted.	Remove by hand or spray with malathion if infestation is severe.
Tarsonemid mite	Outer leaves curl up, stems rot, flowers and buds wither.	Remove damaged foliage straight away in attempt to save plant. No effective chemicals available.
Red spider mite	Spin webs on the underside of leaves, but are difficult to see with the naked eye. Suck the sap from leaves, which become mottled and pale. Plants may die.	Maintain correct humidity and watering levels. Isolate infected plants and spray with malathion.
Scale insects	Live on underside of leaves, sucking the sap and weakening the plant. They excrete a sticky substance.	Scrape off insects, wash the plant with clear water and spray with malathion.
Whitefly	Pale green scales of young whitefly suck sap and produce sticky substance which weakens and distorts plants. Adult whitefly fly off when plant is touched.	Remove worst affected leaves, wash plant with clear water and spray with malathion.
Mealy bugs	Lives on underside of leaves. Young look like small flattened pale brown discs, adults are protected by a cottonwool-like fluff. Worst on necks of bulbs. Plants turn yellow and become deformed.	Scrape off with sharp blade. Wash plant with methylated spirits. Spray with malathion. **NB** malathion is not recommended for use on ferns or pileas. Use derris powder instead.

DISEASES	SYMPTOMS	REMEDY
Grey mould (botrytis)	Grey furry covering on leaves, stems and other parts. Infected parts rot and fall off, and the disease spreads rapidly if conditions are too cool and moist.	Improve cultural conditions, remove affected plants, and spray with a systemic fungicide.
Mildew	Patches of white powder, usually on leaves and stems, sometimes on flowers. Begonias are particularly susceptible if dry at the roots when the atmosphere is moist and warm.	Remove affected tissue and spray with benomyl.
Sooty mould	Black patches on leaves and stems which have been damaged by sticky excretions of pests.	Sponge leaves clean with tepid water. Deal with the insects.
Azalea gall	Fungus causing thickening of the leaves, which are covered with a whitish bloom.	Remove affected parts by hand as soon as seen.
Root rot	Waterlogged soil causes fungal decay. Leaves wilt and plant may quickly die.	Remove affected roots if possible.
Leaf spot	Damp conditions cause fungal decay. Small brown spots appear which soon cover all leaf surface.	Remove affected parts. Spray with benomyl.
Basal rot	Whole plant wilts, due to overwatering, poor ventilation, excessively high temperatures.	Remove affected part if possible, otherwise discard plant.

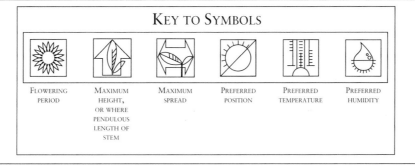

KEY TO SYMBOLS

FLOWERING PERIOD · MAXIMUM HEIGHT, OR WHERE PENDULOUS LENGTH OF STEM · MAXIMUM SPREAD · PREFERRED POSITION · PREFERRED TEMPERATURE · PREFERRED HUMIDITY

FOLIAGE PLANTS

When early improvements in domestic heating made it possible to grow tender plants indoors, foliage plants (including palms and ferns) were the first to be used to decorate the garden rooms and conservatories of the privileged in the Victorian era. With characteristic zeal plant-gatherers sought as much variety and rarity as they could; by the end of the Edwardian age any conservatory worthy of the name was full to bursting. Social and economic changes may have swept all that away, but we still have the vast choice of plants at our disposal, beautifying and enlivening our homes and workplaces.

SHAPE AND FORM

Where once sheer quantity was the aim, now – for practical reasons as well as matters of taste – foliage plants are chosen for their individual qualities or for their effect in judiciously placed small groups. A pretty tiled fireplace made redundant by central heating, a broad landing lit by a skylight, a deep windowsill with a dull aspect: all are vacant spots which can be transformed by an arrangement of foliage plants.

A wide variety of leaf forms create a jungle effect in a conservatory.

When planning a foliage group, take into account how much individual species differ in shape, size and the texture of their leaves. They may be sword-shaped like chlorophytum; lobed like a fatshedera, oval like a maranta, circular like a saxifrage – there are many more variations. The leaves of a fatsia are huge and glossy; those of the fittonia tiny and soft.

COLOUR

A challenge comes with blending colours, too. Not all foliage plants are green, and those that are display a brilliant range of shades. Compare the fresh apple green of the plectranthus with the deep green of a healthy *Ficus elastica*. A group made up of peperomia species will offer greens of every hue, leaves of numerous shapes, some smooth and some deeply corrugated. Variegated leaves are those which are marked with a colour other than green, often white, cream, pink, silver or gold. It may be evident as a stripe, as in chlorophytum, for example; as an edging to the leaf, as in *Peperomia magnoliifolia* 'Variegata' or as irregular blotches, as in *Scindapsus aureus*. Hypoestes leaves are spotted pale pink; in fittonias the leaf veins take colour, either pink or cream. Beautiful colours and markings are seen on the leaves of the varieties of *Maranta leuconeura* and its relatives ctenanthe and calathea. In *Calathea picturata* 'Argentea' almost the whole leaf area is silver, with green just at the edges. Perhaps the most spectacular variegations are to be seen on the huge leaves of *Begonia rex* hybrids, splashed and banded variously red, purple, pink, silver and shades of green. They are rivalled by the caladium; its heart-shaped leaves, up to 37cm/15in long, may be entirely white, lightly veined green, or green splashed with vivid pink. There are a handful of plants which have completely abandoned all thought of green, such as *Iresine herbstii*, a startling red, and *Setcreasea purpurea*, rich purple. In a mixed group one of these two would make a good focal point. Some might find the colours too strong without a background of green, but if your taste is for the unusual, why not?

GROUPING PLANTS FOR INTEREST

A successful indoor planting scheme takes into account the same design principles applied to a herbaceous border: plants for height at the back, bushy medium-size specimens in the centre and miniatures or trailers at the front. A line of erect growers would look too formal, while trailers all together (unless in a hanging basket) might look doleful. For height choose climbers, such as *Cissus rhombifolia* or *Philodendron scandens*. The choice of middle height plants is huge and includes toleima, pilea, peperomia, hypoestes and maranta. *Ficus pumila* is one of the prettiest trailers. Others are *Peperomia scandens*, *Saxifraga stolonifera*, plectranthus and that popular pair, tradescantia and zebrina (as well as their colourful cousin, the aforementioned setcreasea). All of these are excellent for hanging baskets.

If you have space for several hanging baskets, do not feel they all have to be at the same level. Try varying the length of the strings to make a composite display of different plants. This idea works well with plants of different sizes – for example *Philodendron bipinnatifidum*, at 90cm/3ft high, and some of the larger ferns. Check that your ceiling joists will take the weight of several baskets before you organize your display.

An important consideration when grouping plants together is to use a selection which, as far as possible, have similar needs in terms of light, temperature and humidity. Set in a group, plants trap moisture under the leaves and help keep humidity high. It is also more convenient to water and feed all your plants at once, especially if you are short of time.

In terms of low maintenance, a bottle garden is hard to beat. Traditional bottle gardens with a stopper are ideal for moisture-loving plants which do not need full sun. Any type of attractive glass container will do as long as the neck is wide enough. Larger bottles like carboys are extremely effective. Small or slow-growing plants are essential. Some good subjects are pileas, fittonia, *Ficus pumila* and *Hedera helix*. The ferns *Adiantum capillus-veneris* and pteris also do well.

PLANTING UP A BOTTLE GARDEN

Work out the arrangement of your plants before you begin. Do not plant them too close together, as they will grow to cover any bare patches.

You will need three bamboo canes. Using twine or wire, fix to one a small spoon, to one a small fork, and wedge the third into an empty cotton reel. Also useful is a long-handled artist's paintbrush. Make up a potting mixture of equal quantities of loam or soil-based compost, sand and peat. Add a small quantity of crushed charcoal. A funnel or a piece of strong paper rolled into a cone is needed to pour the compost into the container. For watering, use a small watering can or a length of narrow plastic tubing.

The container must be clean and dry to start. Using the funnel, pour in enough mixture to come one-third of the way up the glass. Firm it down evenly with the cotton reel. Make holes for each of the plants using the spoon and fork. Working with one plant at a time, remove it from its pot and shake excess compost from the roots. Work from the outside towards the middle. You can drop the plants through the hole and then pick them up with the spoon and fork, or lower them in between two canes, chopstick fashion, or use a long piece of wire with a hook on the end. Set each plant upright in its hole. With the spoon, cover the roots with compost and firm it down with the cotton reel. When all the plants are in place, add water by pouring it down the sides of the container. This will clean the glass at the same time. The compost should be moist, not saturated. Any excess cannot drain away, so go carefully. Specks of compost on the leaves can be removed with the paintbrush.

Put the stopper in. If condensation appears all over the glass within the next few days, remove the stopper for a while. You may have to do this three or four times before the balance is right. A little condensation near the top is healthy and will come and go. No condensation at all means you should add water.

The bottle garden may need a light watering after some months, but otherwise can be left alone (apart from dusting the outside). The plants will probably have outgrown their space after three years and the garden can be re-made.

ACORUS

| 45cm/18in | 20cm/8in | medium | 4.5°C/40°F | high |

The delicate, grassy leaves of *Acorus gramineus* rise in a close fan like those of an iris from a rhizome set just below the surface of the compost. They are best appreciated in a grouping of foliage plants where their grace and height contrast well with bushy or trailing specimens.

GENERAL CARE Acoruses are marsh plants, and the roots must never dry out. Grow in soil-based compost and stand the pots in saucers of pebbles kept constantly under water. In spring and summer, feed every 2 weeks with liquid fertilizer. Spray the leaves, using a fine spray, on hot days. The plants can tolerate direct sunlight if it is filtered through a fine curtain. Repot in spring if the fan of leaves touches the side of the pot. Once the plants have reached a 12.5cm/5in pot they should be divided into smaller sections.

PROPAGATION By division in spring or summer.

VARIETIES *A. g. variegatus*, leaves striped with white; *A. g. pusillus*, attractive dwarf form at 7.5cm/3in.

POSSIBLE PROBLEMS Generally trouble-free.

ASPIDISTRA

| 50cm/20in | 60cm/24in | medium | 5°C/41°F | low |

Dubbed 'the cast-iron plant' by the Victorians because of its stoic constitution, *Aspidistra elatior* is indeed an extremely accommodating plant. Its leathery, glossy leaves are dark green, growing in a tightly formed cluster on short stems. A mature aspidistra in an old jardinière looks very dignified in a hallway or on a deep windowsill (out of direct sunlight, which will scorch the leaves).

GENERAL CARE Aspidistras need some attention, in spite of their reputation. Grow in soil-based compost and keep watered all year, so that the compost is just moist. Broken crocks at the bottom of the pot will assist good drainage. Feed every 2 weeks in spring and summer with liquid fertilizer. The plants are happy in cool or warm rooms. Repot in spring only when over-crowding demands it, upgrading to a pot one size larger. Once a mature plant reaches the largest pot you have room for, simply top-dress in spring (*see p. 14*).

PROPAGATION Remove suckers bearing roots in spring and place one to a 10cm/4in pot.

VARIETIES *A. e. variegata*, leaves striped green and white.

POSSIBLE PROBLEMS Brown marks on leaves caused by overwatering.

▨ GENERAL TIP

Acorus gramineus *has been naturalized and growing in East Anglia for 300 years or more, a region in which it is most at home in the wet area at the margins of ponds and similar water features. As indoor plants* *they are rather insignificant on their own unless clumps of growth are large. Plunged in moss in mixed plantings they offer pleasing contrast to other foliage.*

▨ CARE TIP

The unusual flowers are produced at soil level and often go unnoticed as a result. Red spider mites can have very debilitating effect on aspidistras, turning leaves brown and crisp.

BEGONIA LUXURIANS

| 60cm/24in | 60cm/24in | bright | 10°C/50°F | high |

Begonia luxurians is a fibrous-rooted plant with the slightly hairy leaves which characterize the 'hirsute' begonias. Its pale green leaves may be divided into as many as 17 pointed leaflets, giving them the appearance of palm leaves. The stems are tinged with red. No named varieties are available.

GENERAL CARE Treat fibrous-rooted begonias in the same way as rhizomatous types like *Begonia rex* hybrids. While both kinds need humidity, they need less water when resting during the winter. Let the top half of the compost dry out between waterings at this time.

PROPAGATION Take 10cm/4in tip cuttings in late spring and root in a compost of equal parts of peat and sand at a temperature of 18-21°C/64-70°F.

POSSIBLE PROBLEMS Powdery mildew; yellowing of leaves if too dry, overwatered or too cold.

BEGONIA REX

| 30cm/12in | 38cm/15in | bright | 13°C/55°F | high |

The group of hybrids derived from *Begonia rex* are prized for their magnificent leaves. Roughly heart-shaped and slightly hairy, they reach as much as 30cm/12in in length and are almost as wide. The wrinkled texture and toothed edges emphasize the beautiful colours in shades of green, silver and pink or red, often with a metallic sheen. *Begonia rex* grows from a rhizome, which rests near the surface and sends down roots at several points.

GENERAL CARE Grow in a peat-based mixture with a layer of broken crocks at the bottom for good drainage. Set half-pots in trays of moist pebbles to maintain humidity and water the plants moderately during the growth period. At this time feed every 2 weeks with liquid fertilizer and keep at normal room temperatures. Bright light without direct sunlight is essential in order to maintain foliage colour. Repot overcrowded specimens in spring. Eventually old plants will need to be replaced.

PROPAGATION By leaf cuttings in late spring.

VARIETIES *B. r.* 'President', green and silver; 'Merry Christmas', red, pink, silver and green.

POSSIBLE PROBLEMS Powdery mildew; yellowing of leaves if too dry, overwatered or too cold.

▤ DESIGN TIP

Something of a connoisseur's plant and one that will be difficult to obtain. Graceful, open plants on stout stems are fine as background subjects for setting off lesser plants in groups

▤ PROPAGATION TIP

To be able to propagate new plants is something of an achievement among the enthusiastic growers of houseplants. Important needs are a heated propagating case and plants with firm and

unblemished leaves. Take off a good leaf, reduce the petiole to one inch, cut through the veins in several places and rest the leaf on peat and sand mix with colour side up (see page 15, Fig 3).

CALADIUM

60cm/24in	60cm/24in	bright	13°C/55°F	high

The extraordinary foliage of *Caladium bicolor*, native to tropical America, is not produced without some care. Given suitable conditions, this plant bears large, paper-thin leaves of silvery green, marked with white, magenta or dark green.

GENERAL CARE Grow in a peat-based mixture with a 2.5cm/1in layer of drainage material at the bottom of the pot. During the growing period maintain a temperature between 18 and 24°C/65 and 75°F. Mist-spray three times a day. Stand the pots in a tray of pebbles kept constantly moist. Feed with a liquid fertilizer at half-strength every 2 weeks. Avoid cold draughts at all costs. When the leaves die down in autumn, reduce the amount of water gradually. A dormant period of at least 5 months follows. Keep the tubers in their pots away from the light and do not let them dry out. Repot in the spring, placing them at about their own depth below the surface of the compost, and restore normal growing conditions.

PROPAGATION Detach and replant offsets when repotting.

VARIETIES *C. b. macrophyllum*, deep green, spotted white and rose-pink; *C. b. regale*, pointed bright green leaves edged purple, spotted white; *C. b. devosianum*, green edged crimson, spotted white and pink.

POSSIBLE PROBLEMS Leaves turn brown and wither if temperatures are too low.

CARE TIP

With leaves that are white with green venation the variety C. candidum is almost translucent – the movement of a hand being clearly seen on the opposite side of the plant. Purchased tubers should be firm and free of blemishes and when starting growth in late winter it is important that high temperature prevails, in excess of 20°C (68°F) if possible. Keep just moist to begin with.

CALATHEA PICTURATA

20cm/8in	30cm/12in	medium	10°C/50°F	moderate

The leaves of *Calathea picturata* are similar in shape to those of its relative the zebra plant, but much smaller and predominantly silver in colour, with a bright green margin. They are deep red underneath, and this feature is easy to appreciate as the leaves are held almost upright on short stems.

GENERAL CARE Treat as *C. zebrina*. As an alternative to a peat-based mixture, you can use a mixture of soil-based compost and leaf-mould or peat in the ratio 2:1. In this case feeding during the active growth period can be reduced to once weekly.

PROPAGATION Divide and replant overcrowded plants in late spring.

POSSIBLE PROBLEMS Generally trouble-free.

CARE TIP

The leaves of C. p. Argentea have, as the name suggests, a glowing silver centre with a dark green margin – colouring seen in few other plants. As an ornament in the living room they are not likely to do well – needing warmth and humidity to succeed. A growing case, or a window extended outwards in the form of a large bay with sliding glass door to the room can be ideal.

CALATHEA ZEBRINA

| 38cm/15in | 60cm/24in | medium | 10°C/50°F | moderate |

Calatheas are closely related to marantas, and are sometimes difficult to tell apart. Most varieties have roughly oval leaves, prominently marked with stripes or with a broad margin of colour. *Calathea zebrina* (*above*) is commonly known as the zebra plant, because of the strong contrast between the leaves' pale green veins and midribs against soft-textured bright green. Each leaf rises from a stiff stalk on which it is held at a pronounced, almost horizontal, angle.

GENERAL CARE Grow in a peat-based potting mixture. When plants are actively growing keep the mixture constantly moist with cooled boiled water or rainwater. Feed with liquid fertilizer 3 times a week. The ideal temperature is 16-22°C/60-70°F. Stop feeding and reduce the amount of water during the winter resting period. Repot one size up annually in late spring.

PROPAGATION Divide and replant overcrowded plants in late spring. Enclose each small pot in a plastic bag until new roots have formed.

SPECIES *Calathea makoyana* (peacock plant); 30cm/12in leaves on long stems, marked green, silver and deep red depending on quality of light.

POSSIBLE PROBLEMS Generally trouble-free.

CHLOROPHYTUM

| 25cm/10in | 60cm/24in | bright | 7°C/45°F | moderate |

Variously labelled *Chlorophytum capense*, *C. comosum* and *C. elatum*, the well-known spider plant is deservedly popular. Its long, grass-like leaves have a central white stripe. Each plant produces new plantlets at the end of narrow arching stems. They look their best in hanging baskets or on tall plant stands.

GENERAL CARE Chlorophytums are not difficult to cultivate. Grow in a soil-based compost and keep constantly just moist in spring and summer. During the winter resting period the compost should not be allowed to dry out completely. Feed mature plants all year round with liquid fertilizer every 2 weeks. Repot whenever the mass of fleshy roots has pushed up out of the compost.

PROPAGATION Peg young plants into small pots of potting compost and sever from the parent plant when rooted. Alternatively detach plantlets with little roots from the parent and place in water until the roots are 2.5cm/1in long. Pot up in soil-based compost.

VARIETIES *C. c. variegatum*, most common form, green leaves with central white band.

POSSIBLE PROBLEMS Generally trouble-free.

▪ GENERAL TIP

One of the testing plants that require skill and adequate temperature to maintain, but rewarding. Excellent subjects for growing in a heated plant growing case with moisture control.

▪ CARE TIP

The ubiquitous 'Spider Plant' is frequently neglected by being underfed and potted on too seldom, while attention to both of these aspects can produce superb plants for hanging containers.

CISSUS

3m/10ft	1.2m/4ft	medium	4.5°C/40°F	moderate

Cissus rhombifolia (formerly *Rhoicissus rhomboidea*) is commonly known as grape ivy. This beautiful plant is closely related to the true grape vine, and climbs by means of tendrils at about 60-90cm/2-3ft a year. Regular cutting back, however, will keep it bushy. The green, glossy leaves are composed of 3 diamond-shaped leaflets.

GENERAL CARE Grow in a soil-based compost and set in good light. Most types of cissus are tolerant of wide variations in light, but dislike direct sunlight. A tall stake is necessary on which to train the exuberant growth. Water well during active growth, allowing the top layer of compost to dry out between applications. Feed every 2 weeks from spring until late autumn. The ideal temperature while growing is around 16-18°C/ 60-65°F. Cut back the leading growths by one-third in spring to keep the shape attractive. Repot in early spring until a pot size of 25cm/10in has been reached. Thereafter top-dress annually in spring.

PROPAGATION Take 10cm/4in tip cuttings in spring and root in a compost of equal parts peat and sand at a temperature of 16-18°C/61-64°F.

VARIETIES *C. r.* 'Ellen Danica', a graceful plant with leaves more deeply cut and glossier than the species.

POSSIBLE PROBLEMS Red spider mite in dry atmospheres.

▦ DESIGN TIP

Adaptable plants in that they may be used as either climbers or trailers. In the latter capacity they are seen to best effect when growing as a single subject in a hanging container of reasonable size. Alternatively, a trellis framework can be placed in the growing pot or attached to the wall adjacent to the growing container to allow the plant to cling naturally.

CODIAEUM

90cm/3ft	60cm/24in	bright	16°C/60°F	high

There is a tremendous variation in leaf form and colour among the codiaeums, or crotons as they are commonly called. Red, yellow and green and varying combinations of these colours are flamboyantly displayed on leathery leaves that may be oval, lanceolate or deeply cut. In the variety 'Spirale' they are even twisted.

GENERAL CARE These handsome plants require at least 2 hours of direct sunshine every day to maintain leaf colour. Normal room temperatures are sufficient. Grow in a soil-based compost, water plentifully during the growth period and feed every 2 weeks. Set the pots on trays of pebbles kept just moist. Do not let the compost dry out completely in the dormant period. Repot each spring. When the largest convenient pot size has been reached, simply top-dress with fresh compost (*see p. 14*).

PROPAGATION Take 15cm/6in tip cuttings in early spring. To stop the flow of milky sap from the stems, plunge the ends in water. Insert the cuttings singly in 6cm/2½in pots of equal parts peat and sand.

VARIETIES *Codiaeum variegatum pictum* 'Madame Mayne' (*above*), deeply cut leaves, golden yellow when young, green veined yellow in maturity; 'Reidii', oval, curved, wavy leaves, mid-green striped cream ageing to deep pink.

▦ CARE TIP

In dry and hot conditions a major enemy of this plant is the minute red spider mite which is flesh-coloured rather than red, so difficult to detect. Use suitable systemic insecticide as a precaution.

COLEUS

| 45cm/18in | 30cm/12in | bright | 13°C/55°F | high |

Popularly known as the flame nettle, *Coleus blumei* is a popular house plant valued for its beautifully coloured leaves and for its usefulness in plant groups. The delicate leaves are shaped like those of the nettle (to which it is not related) but are invariably very brightly marked. As these plants are easily raised from cuttings, they are usually discarded after one season.

GENERAL CARE Grow in a soil-based compost and keep it thoroughly moist at all times. Maximum bright light, including 2-3 hours of direct sunlight daily, is very important. Coleuses like warmth, but at temperatures above 18°C/65°F maintain humidity by standing the pots in trays of pebbles kept constantly damp. Feed every 2 weeks during the growing period and repot every 2 months so that the roots have room to spread. Pinch out the growing tips regularly to encourage bushy growth.

PROPAGATION Take 7.5cm/3in tip cuttings in the autumn and place directly in potting compost in a warm position.

VARIETIES There are innumerable good named varieties.

POSSIBLE PROBLEMS Leaves fall if the compost is allowed to dry out, and the colour will fade in inadequate light.

CTENANTHE

| 90cm/3ft | 45cm/18in | bright | 16°C/61°F | moderate |

Ctenanthes belong to the same family as marantas and calatheas. The matt leaves are rather more slender and pointed than those of its relatives. Splashed irregularly with cream, they are purple on the underside. Ctenanthes combine well with other plants in a mixed display.

GENERAL CARE Grow in a mixture of soil-based compost and leaf-mould. Set in bright light, not direct sunlight, at normal room temperatures. Stand pots on dampened pebbles and water regularly during active growth. Give a liquid feed every 2 weeks. Repot each spring. When the largest convenient pot size has been reached, simply top-dress annually (*see p. 14*).

PROPAGATION Detach the basal offsets from the parent and replant immediately in the recommended growing medium.

VARIETIES *Ctenanthe oppenheimiana* 'Tricolor' and 'Burle Marx' (*above*), known as the never-never plant, with pointed leaves 25cm/10in long on slender stalks.

POSSIBLE PROBLEMS Leaves curl up if exposed to over-bright light.

▦ GENERAL TIP

Plants that are raised from seed will not be difficult to establish but these are not the best sort of coleus to acquire. There are also named kinds, such as C. 'Pineapple Queen' and 'Paisley Shawl' that are very much superior in respect of colour, growth and general appearance. Bought at the start of the season they need regular potting and feeding to prosper.

▦ DESIGN TIP

Ctenanthe oppenheimiana Tricolor *is a fine plant if given modest warmth and shade from direct sun. Grown in pan type containers these are excellent among other plants when employed as ground cover.*

CYPERUS

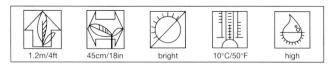

| 1.2m/4ft | 45cm/18in | bright | 10°C/50°F | high |

Cyperus alternifolius (*above*) bears its leaves at the top of the stem, radiating outwards like the spokes of a wheel. Because of this formation it is commonly called umbrella plant, and the watery connotations are appropriate – this plant is aquatic, and needs to have its pot sitting in a shallow tray constantly filled with water.

GENERAL CARE Grow in pots of soil-based compost set in full or filtered sunlight. Normal room temperatures are suitable. Water frequently and spray mist the leaves daily in an upward direction. Feed every month with liquid fertilizer when actively growing. Cyperus grow quickly and will need repotting whenever the clumps become overcrowded.

PROPAGATION Divide the roots in early spring. Do not plant new sections too deep in their new pots. Alternatively detach a spray of bracts with a short length of stem and keep in water until roots appear. Pot up in the recommended mixture.

VARIETIES *C. a.* 'Gracilis', dwarf variety with darker green leaves; 'Variegatus', foliage striped white when young, ageing to green.

POSSIBLE PROBLEMS Generally trouble-free.

DIEFFENBACHIA

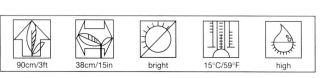

| 90cm/3ft | 38cm/15in | bright | 15°C/59°F | high |

All dieffenbachias are poisonous, with very bitter sap. The common name, dumb cane, refers to the fact that loss of speech follows if any part of the plant is placed in the mouth. These negative qualities have not prevented dieffenbachias becoming popular houseplants. They are much admired for their large, handsome leaves, beautifully marked cream and green.

GENERAL CARE Grow in a soil-based compost. Set the plants where they can enjoy bright, filtered light during the growing period, with direct sunlight in the winter. Stand the pots in trays of pebbles kept moist and water so that the mixture is constantly damp. Feed every 2 weeks except when dormant. Repot annually in spring.

PROPAGATION Take 10cm/4in tip cuttings in early summer, insert in a compost of equal parts of peat and sand and keep the pots in plastic bags until the cuttings have rooted. Alternatively take cuttings from the main stem; the parent plant can be discarded but may well break into new growth from the base.

VARIETIES *Dieffenbachia picta* 'Exotica' (*above*), deep green leaves blotched white and yellow; 'Rudolph Roehrs' ('Roehrsii'), creamy leaves veined white; 'Bausii', leaves particoloured dark and light green, spotted silver.

POSSIBLE PROBLEMS Generally trouble-free.

▨ CARE TIP

These are among the easiest indoor plants to manage and ideal for the person who is heavy handed with water. In fact, water is the name of the game in respect of cyperus and they do make excellent poolside features if one is fortunate enough to have a conservatory that can accommodate a small pool. In larger pools they are fine as island plants on a raised mound in the water.

▨ PROPAGATION TIP

Success with propagation is always a bonus, and with this plant older stems can be cut into sections with an eye and laid horizontally, half buried in peaty mixture with the eye uppermost.

DIZYGOTHECA

1.2m/4ft	45cm/18in	bright	15°C/60°F	high

Dizygothecas, or false aralias, are elegant plants with narrow, serrated leaflets radiating from the tips of slender stalks. They are beautiful enough to stand alone – especially if planted 3 to a pot – but can also be used in a collection of tropical plants to add height and grace.

GENERAL CARE Grow in a soil-based compost and set the plants in bright light, not direct sunlight. Steadily maintained humidity is important. Stand the pots in saucers of pebbles kept moist, and do not let the compost become either waterlogged or dried out. Feed with liquid fertilizer every 2 weeks in the growing period. Pot on every other year in spring.

PROPAGATION New plants are normally raised from seed.

SPECIES *Dizygotheca elegantissima* (finger or false aralia, *above*), young leaves copper-coloured ageing to dark green, almost black; *D. veitchii*, wider leaflets of bright green, deep red beneath.

POSSIBLE PROBLEMS Plants become spindly in conditions that are less than ideal.

DRACAENA

1.2m/4ft	60cm/24in	bright	13°C/55°F	high

There are a number of dracaenas, all of them striking plants and well deserving of a place in a conservatory or sunny room. *Dracaena fragrans* has glossy, strap-like leaves radiating from the centre. As the plant matures the stem lengthens, bearing the rosette of leaves at the top.

GENERAL CARE Grow in soil-based compost and water well during the period of growth. Give a liquid feed every 2 weeks. Bright light, though not direct sunlight, is essential. The ideal temperature is in the range 18-23°C/65-75°F. Stand the pots in trays of damp pebbles and spray the foliage from time to time to maintain a high level of humidity. Repot annually in spring.

PROPAGATION Take tip or stem cuttings in spring or summer and root in a compost of equal parts of peat and sand at a temperature of 21-24°C/70-75°F.

VARIETIES *D. f.* 'Massangeana', dark green leaves with a golden central band; 'Lindenii', gold and green leaves edged gold.

POSSIBLE PROBLEMS Leaf drop in low temperatures; scale insects on leaves.

▓ GENERAL TIP

Dizygotheca elegantissima is never an easy plant to care for and one that will almost inevitably lose lower leaves as the main stem hardens with age. An interesting feature of this plant is the manner in which it changes character as the stem increases in height – the delicate filigreed leaves give way to much coarser leaves that are more typical of the araliaceae family to which it belongs.

▓ DESIGN TIP

Many fine plants here, almost all of erect growth – a feature that is very effective when groups of the same or mixed varieties are arranged in a large container or in decorative pots at floor level.

ELETTARIA

| 60cm/24in | 60cm/24in | low | 7°C/45°F | low |

Native to India, *Elettaria cardamom* is the chief commercial source of cardamom seeds, one of the most expensive spices in the world. This rhizomatous plant bears numerous thick stems with pointed, slender mid-green leaves. It has a dense, bushy appearance and is useful for hallways and other poorly lit rooms. There are no named varieties.

GENERAL CARE Grow in a soil-based compost. Normal room temperatures and poor or moderate light are best; the leaves lose their colour in direct sunlight. Water moderately and give a liquid feed every 2 weeks when the plant is in active growth. The stems of elettarias soon fill the pot, necessitating repotting, which can be done at any time except when the plant is dormant. When they become too large for the largest suitable pot, the plants should be divided.

PROPAGATION Divide and repot plants in spring. Each clump of stems must be attached to a good piece of rhizome and roots.

VARIETIES *E. c.* 'Variegata' (*above*).

POSSIBLE PROBLEMS Leaves turn brown at temperatures below 13°C/55°F during the active growth period.

▓ GENERAL TIP

A ginger plant that has been available spasmodically over the years almost from the introduction of houseplants way back in the early 1950s, but it has never achieved great popularity. If plants are not available from normal sources, it may well be possible to obtain rhizomes from the exotic food stores.

× FATSHEDERA

| 1.2m/4ft | 60cm/24in | shade | 4°C/37°F | low |

The hybrid *Fatshedera lizei* (*above*) has characteristics of both its parents: the tough constitution of *Hedera helix hibernica* (Irish ivy) and the glossy, handsome leaves of *Fatsia japonica*. Fatshedera leaves may be up to 20cm/8in wide and are best appreciated when several plants are grown in one pot, giving a bushy appearance.

GENERAL CARE Grow in a soil-based compost. As the plants grow they need the support of thin stakes to prevent them toppling over. It is advisable to place these in the pot while plants are still young. Light shade is best, but the variegated type needs brighter light (not direct sunlight) to maintain its markings. Fatshederas are not fussy about room temperature, but the variegated type needs to be at a minimum of 15°C/59°F at all times. Water moderately and feed every 2 weeks when in active growth. Repot annually in spring, providing longer stakes if necessary.

PROPAGATION Take 10cm/4in tip cuttings in spring and root in a compost of equal parts of peat and sand.

VARIETIES *F. l.* 'Variegata', slower growing variety with white splashes on the leaves.

POSSIBLE PROBLEMS Red spider mite.

▓ GENERAL TIP

Like its parents the fatsia (aralia) and hedera (ivy) this is a reasonably hardy plant when grown out of doors – perhaps when it has become leggy and less attractive indoors.

FATSIA

| 1.5m/5ft | 1.2m/4ft | bright | 4-5°C/40°F | moderate |

Fatsia japonica, the false castor oil plant, is an imposing specimen with large, green, dark green, glossy leaves. Native to Japan, it is hardy to enough to grow outdoors, where it may exceed the dimensions given above. As a potted house plant, it usually reaches about 90cm/3ft. Small white flowers appear in autumn, but to preserve the handsome foliage it is best to remove the buds.

GENERAL CARE Grow in a soil-based compost kept thoroughly moist during the summer, and give a liquid feed every two weeks. Fatsias need good light, not direct sunlight, and prefer cooler temperatures, ideally about 15°C/59°F; over 18°C/64°F the leaves begin to flop. Pinch out the growing tips of young plants to encourage bushy growth. Clean the leaves by sponging them with tepid water. In the rest period, keep the compost just moist. Repotting may be necessary during the growing season as fatsias are fast growers. The final pot size will be 25cm/10in, after which simply topdress with fresh compost annually.

PROPAGATION Detach suckers, if any, in early spring, and pot up individually in potting compost.

VARIETIES *F. j. variegata* (*above*): leaves tinged white; *F. j. Moseri*: leaves larger than the species, but the plant more compact.

POSSIBLE PROBLEMS Leaves shrivel in dry, hot atmosphere.

▦ SPECIAL CARE TIP

The variegated form with cream blotches or edges to the leaves grows more slowly and is much less resistant to cold. If the temperature falls below freezing, it is likely to shed its leaves in winter. For this reason and because of its attractive light-coloured leaves it makes an ideal subject for a well-used room indoors.

FICUS BENJAMINA

| 2m/6ft | 90cm/3ft | bright | 13°C/55°F | moderate |

The ficus family includes an enormous variety of handsome foliage plants. *Ficus benjamina (above)*, the weeping fig, has some of the grace of *F. pumila* combined with the stature of *F. elastica*. It is ideal for the corner of a room, as it does not need to be rotated towards the light, but its glossy oval leaves on slightly drooping branches look good in any setting. There are no named varieties.

GENERAL CARE Grow in soil-based compost, using a pot that looks too small for the plant (ficus like their roots to be cramped). Water moderately, allowing the top half of the compost to dry out between waterings. Give a liquid feed every two weeks when in active growth. Good light, not direct sunlight, is essential. *F. benjamina* can thrive in cool or warm rooms, though sudden changes in temperature will be damaging. At high temperatures there is an increased risk of attack by red spider mite. Carefully sponge the leaves with tepid water from time to time to clean them. Repot in spring, but only when the roots are appearing through the drainage hole of the pot.

PROPAGATION Take 7.5cm/3in cuttings of side shoots in early summer. *F. benjamina* may also be increased by air layering.

POSSIBLE PROBLEMS Scale insects; red spider mite.

▦ DESIGN TIP

Some rooms call for a single imposing plant and Ficus benjamina might very well be the answer particularly as it offers elegance and delicacy with significant height and a tree-like habit.

FICUS ELASTICA

2.4m/8ft	90cm/3ft	bright	16°C/60°F	low

Ficus elastica, the rubber plant, is one of the most popular indoor plants. Though potentially very tall, it usually reaches about 1.2m/4ft – stately enough, and classically handsome with oval, shiny dark green leaves.

GENERAL CARE Grow in a soil-based compost, using a pot size that will cramp the roots slightly. Set in full light, out of direct sunlight. Water thoroughly, during the growing period, allowing the compost to dry out slightly between applications. Use cooled boiled water or rainwater if possible. Feed every 2 weeks. Wipe the leaves gently to remove dust. In winter, keep the compost just moist. Pot on in spring if necessary. To encourage a bushy habit, pinch out the growing point. Sap exuding from the wound can be stopped with powdered charcoal.

PROPAGATION Air-layering is the best method, but is difficult for the amateur.

VARIETIES *F. e.* 'Decora' (*above left*), best-known plain-leaved variety; 'Black Prince' (*above centre*), very dark green leaves; 'Variegata' (*above right*), slightly narrower leaves edged yellow and with yellow mottling.

POSSIBLE PROBLEMS Leaf drop in low temperatures; scale insects on leaves.

FICUS PUMILA

60cm/24in	60cm/24in	shade	7°C/45°F	high

In contrast to its relative the rubber plant, *Ficus pumila* – the creeping fig – climbs or trails on thin, wiry stems. Its diminutive leaves are bright green and attractively heart-shaped. It is best set in an arrangement with other plants where humidity is raised and where its low habit of growth can offset taller, bushier specimens.

GENERAL CARE Grow in a peat-based compost and keep evenly moist throughout the year – the leaves are too thin to retain much moisture. Pinch out the growing tips regularly to encourage a spreading habit. *F. pumila* likes shade and cool temperatures. In the growing period feed every 2 weeks with liquid fertilizer. Pot on when absolutely necessary in spring; all ficus like to have their roots rather cramped.

PROPAGATION Take 15cm/6in tip cuttings in spring and root in a compost of equal parts of peat and sand at a temperature of 16-18°C/61-64°F.

VARIETIES *F. p. variegata*, green leaves spotted cream; this variety needs slightly higher temperatures and better light than the species, or it will revert to plain green.

POSSIBLE PROBLEMS Red spider mite; mealy bug.

■ PROPAGATION TIP

There have been many improvements in the rubber plant since the original F. elastica *came into favour, but they all seem to lose lower leaves with age. Top sections of such plants can be air-layered by removing a leaf, cutting upwards through the node and putting a match into the wound to prevent it re-sealing – wet moss and plastic cover should ensure rooting.*

■ DESIGN TIP

The creeping fig is a fine plant for rapidly covering a damp wall in a heated conservatory – roots are self-clinging thus enabling the plant to travel long distances very effectively.

FITTONIA

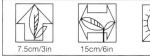 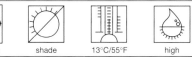

| 7.5cm/3in | 15cm/6in | shade | 13°C/55°F | high |

Fittonias, or snakeskin plants, are one of the prettiest low-growing indoor plants. Their pale green oval leaves, veined in a contrasting colour, completely cover the surface of the growing medium. Site the pots on a low table where this carpet of leaves can be viewed from above.

GENERAL CARE Grow in half-pots of peat-based compost and keep it just moist all the time. Spray the leaves frequently with a fine mist. Feed every 2 weeks with half-strength liquid fertilizer. A steadily maintained temperature of 18°C/65°F is the ideal; cold draughts are deadly. Fittonias like shade when in active growth, but should be moved into natural light during the winter months. It is not usually necessary to repot fittonias.

PROPAGATION Take tip cuttings with 4 pairs of leaves in spring. New plants may also be raised by layering.

VARIETIES *Fittonia verschaffeltii*, olive green leaves 5cm/2in long, veined pinkish-red; *F. argyroneura* 'Snakeskin' (*above*), smaller leaves veined cream; this variety cannot tolerate temperatures lower than 16°C/61°F. *F. a.* 'Nana' is a miniature form which is easier to grow.

POSSIBLE PROBLEMS Leaves shrivel up if conditions are too dry; stems rot if the compost is too wet.

GYNURA

| 90cm/3ft | 45cm/18in | bright | 13°C/55°F | high |

Gynuras are prized for their colourful leaves, dark green but covered in purple hairs so soft they have given rise to the popular name 'velvet plant'. Flowers sometimes appear in spring but should be picked off before they open as the smell is unpleasant. As trailers, gynuras do well in hanging baskets, but they become straggly with age and should be replaced.

GENERAL CARE Grow in soil-based compost and keep it constantly just moist. To maintain humidity stand the pots in trays of moist pebbles, but do not spray the leaves: drops of moisture trapped in the hairs cause brown spots to develop. A few hours of direct sunlight every day helps keep the colours bright and encourages dense growth. Normal room temperatures are satisfactory. Feed every 4 weeks throughout the year. Repot in spring if the plant is still shapely.

PROPAGATION Take tip cuttings in early spring and root in equal parts peat and sand at a temperature of 18-21°C/64-70°F. Place 3 or 4 new plants in a pot for the best effect.

SPECIES *Gynura auriantica*, oval, bright green leaves up to 15cm/6in long, clothed with purple hairs; *G. sarmentosa* (purple passion vine, *above*), twining form with dark green pointed leaves, covered in deep purple hairs. Pinch out the growing tips of this variety regularly.

POSSIBLE PROBLEMS Aphids.

▦ CARE TIP

All of these attractively venated plants are very susceptible to low temperatures – the foliage being paper thin it simply shrivels and dies. A large plant propagator (perhaps with heating cables) can be utilized as a sort of miniature greenhouse to accommodate fittonias and other tender plants – particularly over the winter when plants are more vulnerable

▦ GENERAL TIP

Almost invariably untidy plants, but instantly attractive when seen growing on a windowsill where the sun can be seen shining onto and through their leaves and highlighting the purple effect.

HEDERA

| 90cm/3ft | 90cm/3ft | shade | 7°C/45°F | moderate |

There are numerous varieties of ivy, some of which are best set in mixed groupings while others can stand alone. *Hedera helix* (English ivy) has the characteristic ivy leaf and a branching habit of growth. Since most varieties do best in lightly shaded situations and are tolerant of cool temperatures, they have become very popular as house plants. Self-clinging, all will climb if provided with supports.

GENERAL CARE Grow in a soil-based mixture and water in moderation during the growing period. Variegated types need some sunlight every day. All are accommodating about temperature levels as long as there are no dramatic changes, and over 18°C/65°F humidity should be increased by mist-spraying the foliage. Feed with liquid fertilizer every 2 weeks during the growing period. Move plants to larger pots when roots can be seen protruding through the drainage holes.

PROPAGATION Take cuttings at any time and place in water until roots appear. Pot up in the recommended mixture.

VARIETIES *H. h.* 'Little Eva' (*above*), green leaves edged cream; 'Sagittaefolia', star-shaped, narrow leaves; 'Russell's Gold', golden leaves; 'Discolor', small neat leaves of green mottled with cream and pink.

POSSIBLE PROBLEMS Scale insects.

HYPOESTES

| 45cm/18in | 30cm/12in | bright | 10°C/50°F | moderate |

Among a clutch of popular names, *Hypoestes phyllostachya* has acquired the label 'polka-dot plant', because of the pink and white spots that are liberally distributed over the oval, pointed leaves. If the growing tips are regularly pinched out the plants keep nicely bushy, but eventually become straggly and should be discarded (new plants are easy to raise from seed).

GENERAL CARE Grow in soil-based compost and keep constantly moist (not waterlogged) during the growing season, using cooled boiled water or rainwater if possible. Keep the compost barely moist during the resting period. To keep the attractive leaf markings the best light is bright sunlight filtered through a fine curtain. Normal room temperatures are suitable. Feed every 2 weeks with liquid fertilizer. Repot whenever the roots become overcrowded.

PROPAGATION Sow seed in seed compost in early spring or take 10cm/4in tip cuttings at any time and place in water until roots appear. Pot up in seed compost until large enough to transfer to 10cm/4in pot of soil-based compost.

VARIETIES *H. phyllostachya* 'Splash', similar to the species but with more pronounced pink markings.

POSSIBLE PROBLEMS Generally trouble-free.

▓ DESIGN TIP

Lots of superb kinds to choose from and all natural climbers against a wall – Hedera (ivy) gold heart being an excellent choice for this purpose. Beside the small leaved forms there are those with larger leaves such as H. canariensis which has beautifully marked cream and green variegated foliage. Larger leaved forms need some form of support to twine around.

▓ DESIGN TIP

When choosing plants, take some time to select those that are compact and of the brightest colouring. A group of small plants placed in a shallow container filled with wet moss can be a very attractive feature.

IRESINE

60cm/24in	20cm/8in	bright	13°C/55°F	high

The blood-red colour of its stems and heart-shaped foliage have earned *Iresine herbstii* the common name 'beefsteak plant'. Much used in outdoor bedding schemes, these shrubby plants have become increasingly popular for indoor decoration too.

GENERAL CARE Grow in a soil-based mixture. During the growing season water liberally and feed with liquid fertilizer every 2 weeks. To keep the leaves brightly coloured, several hours of direct sunlight every day are essential. Normal room temperatures are suitable throughout the year. Pinch out the growing tips to encourage a bushy shape. Repot whenever you can see the roots on the surface of the compost.

PROPAGATION Take 7.5cm/3in tip cuttings in spring and place in water until rooted. Pot up in the recommended compost, 3 cuttings to a 7.5cm/3in pot.

VARIETIES *I. h. aureo-reticulata*; red stems, leaves green splashed gold; *I. h. brilliantissima*, deep crimson leaves and stems; *I. h. wallisii*, dwarf variety with dark purple stems and leaves.

POSSIBLE PROBLEMS Aphids; red spider mite.

MARANTA

20cm/8in	15cm/6in	moderate	13°C/55°F	high

Maranta leuconeura is known as the prayer plant because it holds its leaves erect and close together at the end of the day, like praying hands. These are among the most beautiful foliage house plants, with broad oval leaves dramatically marked in regular patterns.

GENERAL CARE Grow in a soil-based compost, using half-pots as marantas are shallow rooting. Keep the compost constantly moist during the growing period, stand the pots in saucers of moist pebbles and spray the leaves regularly, preferably with rainwater. Feed every 2 weeks with liquid fertilizer. Light shade is best, for the leaves fade in direct sunlight, but a constant temperature in the range 18-21°C/65-70°F is required. Keep almost dry over winter and pot on in the spring, grading up one size.

PROPAGATION Divide and replant large clumps in spring.

VARIETIES *M. leuconeura*, slightly downy, pale green leaves marked white and darker green, purple beneath; *M. l.* 'Kerchoveana', larger leaves with red margins and sometimes also spotted red beneath; *M. l.* 'Massangeana' smaller leaves, marked almost black along the midribs, purple beneath.

POSSIBLE PROBLEMS Aphids; red spider mite.

▦ PLANTING TIP

Bright colouring of the blood red leaves of the 'Brilliantissima' variety are seen to best effect when plants are growing on a windowsill that catches the sun – both leaves and stems are red in colour. If used amongst bedding plants during the summer months this is the sort of plant that can be lifted prior to frosts and potted to use as a room plant.

▦ CARE TIP

Tolerant, shade-loving house plants that abhor bright sunlight. Often seen suffering in pots of inadequate size, they are seen to good advantage when growing in shallow pans as groups.

PEPEROMIA

| 30cm/12in | 15cm/6in | shade | 13°C/55°F | moderate |

There are numerous varieties of peperomia, with foliage of different shapes and colours. All types produce a long, thin flower spike, but it is the leaves which are of interest. A grouping of different varieties makes a beautiful display.

GENERAL CARE Grow in a peat-based compost using small containers or hanging baskets – peperomias do not have an extensive root system. Water very sparingly, and feed only once every 4 weeks with half-strength liquid fertilizer. Normal room temperatures are suitable. Pinch out the growing tips to maintain a bushy shape (this will, incidentally, discourage flower production). Repot if necessary in spring, placing a 2.5cm/1in layer of drainage material at the bottom of the pots.

PROPAGATION Take 7.5cm/3in tip cuttings in spring and root in pots of equal parts peat and sand at 18°C/64°F.

SPECIES *Peperomia argyreia* (*above*) shield-shaped leaves borne on long red stalks. *Peperomia magnoliifolia* (desert privet), 15cm/6in long dark green oval leaves. Leaves of the form 'Variegata' are almost completely cream when young, gradually acquiring more green as they age. *P. caperata*, small, heart-shaped dark green leaves tinged purple, with a ridged surface, a low-growing type; the variety 'Emerald Ripple' is particularly compact.

POSSIBLE PROBLEMS Leaf tips turn brown if the temperature drops suddenly.

▨ GENERAL TIP

Many varieties of these are now available – quite enough for one to acquire an interesting collection. Methods of propagation attract considerable interest. The varieties P. caperata *and* P. hederifolia *are prepared from single leaves dibbed into peat and sand, while* P. sandersii *can have its leaves cut into exact quarters to be stood upright in the mix. Bottom heat needed.*

PHILODENDRON

| 1.8m/6ft | 45cm/18in | bright | 10°C/50°F | low |

There are a great number of philodendrons, many of them climbing plants, with beautiful, leathery leaves of differing forms. In the wild – they are native to central and South America – philodendrons clamber up mossy tree trunks, clinging by means of their aerial roots. Not difficult to grow, this rewarding group includes some of the finest foliage plants.

GENERAL CARE Grow in a peat-based compost, watering regularly during the growing period but allowing it to dry out slightly between applications. Give a liquid feed every two weeks. Philodendrons need good light, not direct sunlight, and are happy at normal room temperatures. In the rest period most species – with the exceptions of *P. scandens* – cannot tolerate temperatures lower than 13°C/55°F. At this time the compost should be kept barely moist. Climbing species need a moss-covered stake to support the aerial roots. Repot when the underground roots crowd the pot, at any time except when resting.

PROPAGATION Take 7.5cm/3in tip cuttings in late spring.

SPECIES *P. scandens* (sweetheart plant, *above*): heart-shaped leaves, evergreen, pinch out growing tips regularly; *P. erubescens* 'Burgundy': slow-growing, arrow-shaped leaves copper red when young; *P. selloum*: non-climber with a rosette of large, deeply incised leaves; *P. bipinnatifidum*: only 90cm/3ft tall, leaves heart-shaped when young.

POSSIBLE PROBLEMS Red spider mite.

▨ DESIGN TIP

Philodendrons have two great features which may enable them to make a striking contribution to the look of a room. The first is their propensity for climbing which can be used to great effect for making a screen or for simply enhancing a tall piece of furniture; the second is their dark, glossy leaves which look good against light-coloured woods.

PILEA

30cm/12in	20cm/8in	bright	13°C/55°F	moderate

Pileas are members of the nettle family, but their foliage is much more varied and attractive than that of the familiar weed. Roughly pointed-oval in shape, the leaves are in shades of green marked with silver or bronze and often of a quilted texture. The different types look striking set in groups together.

GENERAL CARE Grow in a peat-based compost kept continuously moist but not waterlogged during the growing period. Stand the pots in saucers or trays of moist pebbles. Give a liquid feed every 2 weeks in summer. Pileas like a warm atmosphere with good light, though not direct sunlight. Turn the pots round from time to time to ensure even growth, and pinch out the growing tips of any overlong shoots. Repotting is not recommended; replace tired plants with new ones grown from cuttings.

PROPAGATION Take 7.5cm/3in tip cuttings in spring.

SPECIES *Pilea cadierei* (aluminium plant), lightly corrugated green leaves splashed silver form a spreading mound; *P. involucrata*, deeply quilted green leaves; those of *Pilea mollis* 'Moon Valley' (*above*) are very light green veined bronze; *P. spruceana* 'Silver Tree', narrow pointed, dark green leaves with a silver central band.

POSSIBLE PROBLEMS Leaves fall in low temperatures.

PLECTRANTHUS

15cm/6in	60cm/24in	bright	13°C/55°F	low

There are around 120 species of Plectranthus many of which make suitable houseplants. Their foliage is similar to the coleus. *Plectranthus fruticosus* is scented and said to keep away moths.

GENERAL CARE Grow in soil-based compost and keep well-watered while in active growth, without actually letting the pots stand in water. Give a liquid feed every 2 weeks during the active growing period. Place the plants where they will receive several hours in direct sunlight every day. They like warmth, thriving in temperatures up to 21°C/70°F if humidity is correspondingly increased. Pinch out the growing tips to prevent the plants becoming straggly. Repotting is not recommended, as the plants are at their best when young and are easily increased by cuttings.

PROPAGATION Take 7.5cm/3in tip cuttings at any time and insert in small pots of the recommended growing medium.

SPECIES *P. oertendahlii*, trailing plant with almost circular leaves 5cm/2in across, bronze-green veined silver; *P. fruticosus* (*above*) bears lilac flowers in large branched racemes; *P. australis* (Swedish ivy), an erect, bushy species with bright green leaves; reaches up to 90cm/3ft in ideal conditions.

POSSIBLE PROBLEMS Generally trouble-free.

▓ GENERAL TIP

Although P. cadierei *is the front runner in terms of popularity the Artillery Plant,* P. muscosa, *is a touch more fascinating. When the seed pods 'explode' they emit a puff of 'smoke'!*

▓ GENERAL TIP

Not a popular plant with commercial suppliers of houseplants, but very adaptable plants that will tolerate much ill treatment and not seem much bothered. Their habit can only be described as sprawling as they are seldom tidy. But it can be an advantage, particularly when plants are seen growing in hanging containers in a location protected from the sun.

Rhoeo

30cm/12in	30cm/12in	moderate	7°C/45°F	moderate

There is only one species of rhoeo, *Rhoeo spathacea* or boat lily, usually sold as *R. discolor*. The pointed, sword-shaped leaves first appear as a rosette, which in time grows to form a short, thick stem from which side shoots arise. These may be removed if preferred and, if they have developed their own roots, used to raise new plants. The leaves are very handsome, green above and rich purple on the undersides.

GENERAL CARE Grow in any good proprietary compost, watered constantly during the period of active growth but kept just moist when dormant. Bright light, not direct sunlight, and a minimum temperature of 16°C/61°F is essential when in growth. Stand the pots in trays of moist pebbles and feed every 2 weeks with liquid fertilizer. Repot annually in spring.

PROPAGATION Detach rooted basal shoots at any time and pot up singly in a mixture of peat and sand. Pot on using the recommended growing medium when firmly rooted.

VARIETIES *R. s.* 'Variegata' syn. 'Vittata', leaves striped golden.

POSSIBLE PROBLEMS Generally trouble-free.

Rhoicissus

1.2m/4ft	60cm/24in	moderate	10°C/50°F	moderate

Commonly known as Cape grape, *Rhoicissus capensis* is a climbing plant which clings to supports such as bamboo canes with simple tendrils. The shiny, fresh green leaves are roughly heat-shaped and may be up to 20cm/8in across.

GENERAL CARE Grow in soil-based compost kept thoroughly moist during the growing period. Give overhead sprays with water and feed every 2 weeks. Rhoicissus tolerate light shade, but a reasonably bright situation out of direct sunlight is preferable. They are happy in cool or warm rooms as long as there are no sudden variations in temperature. Pinch out the growing tips to encourage a bushy shape. Keep the compost barely moist during the winter and repot in spring. When the largest practical pot size has been reached, top dress annually with fresh compost (*see p.14*). Plants that have become too big can be cut right back and will send out new growth. There are no named varieties.

PROPAGATION Take 10cm/4in tip cuttings in spring and root in equal parts peat and sand at 16-18°C/61-64°F.

POSSIBLE PROBLEMS Overwatering causes the leaves to turn yellow, shrivel and fall. Too little water makes the leaves turn brown.

▨ GENERAL TIP

Common names make it easier for some to remember plants but they also lead to confusion – here we have the Boat Lily, but it is also Moses in the Cradle which alludes to the three white flowers in the boat.

▨ CARE TIP

Not a plant for the faint-hearted, the Cape Grape is a prodigious grower that will be quick to fill its allotted space if conditions are in its favour. A framework of some kind for the vigorous growth is almost an essential requirement, and it will be necessary to train the growth to fill gaps at lower level to provide a more attractive feature.

SANSEVIERIA

45cm/18in	15cm/6in	bright	13°C/55°F	moderate

There are a number of sansevierias in common use, with some disagreement about distinction between species. Undoubtedly the most popular is *Sansevieria trifasciata*, generally known as mother-in-law's tongue, with dark green sword-like leaves.

GENERAL CARE Grow in a soil-based mixture to which one-third its volume of horticultural sand has been added to improve drainage. Use a heavy clay pot for upright varieties which may otherwise overbalance. Temperatures can be up to 26°C/80°F for these natives of West Africa, with plenty of light, preferably direct sunlight. Water moderately when in active growth and when resting allow the compost almost to dry out between waterings. Feeding should be stingy: apply half-strength liquid fertilizer every 4 weeks during the growth period only. Repotting is only necessary just before the overcrowded roots threaten to crack their pots. In other years, top-dress lightly with fresh compost (see p.14).

PROPAGATION Detach offsets from the parent rhizome and pot up, or take leaf cuttings and root in equal parts peat and sand at a temperature of 21°C/70°F.

VARIETIES *S. trifasciata* 'Laurentii', leaves edged golden yellow; *S. hahnii*, a rosette-forming species only 15cm/6in high, leaves edged gold or silver depending on variety.

POSSIBLE PROBLEMS Overwatering causes rot, especially if water is left to settle in the middle of the leaves.

■ PROPAGATION TIP

Combination of cold and wet are the arch enemies of this plant. When propagating from 'toes' it is wise to remove the plant from its pot before cutting away the rhizome and its growth.

SAXIFRAGA

23cm/9in	30cm/12in	bright	7°C/45°F	low

The saxifrages are a huge family of garden plants but only one, *Saxifraga stolonifera* (syn. *S. sarmentosa*) is grown as a house plant. It bears roughly circular, furry green leaves up to 10cm/4in across overlapping in an attractive rosette. Its distinction lies in the numerous little plantlets it bears at the end of long, delicate stolons (runners).

GENERAL CARE Grow in soil-based compost kept constantly moist during the growing period, though the pots should not stand in water. Tiny flowers appear in summer; after they have faded the amount of water should gradually be reduced until only enough is given during the rest period to prevent the compost from drying out. One or 2 hours of direct sunlight every day is recommended. As *S. stolonifera* prefers low temperatures – about 15°C/59°F – early morning sun is best. Repot in spring, putting plenty of drainage material in the pots, but do not expect to keep plants indefinitely.

PROPAGATION Detach plantlets from the parent plant and pot up in a 50:50 mixture of peat and sand. Pot on into the standard compost when rooted.

VARIETIES *S. stolonifera* 'Tricolor', small leaves edged cream, turning pink in good light; less vigorous than the species and needs more hours of sunlight.

POSSIBLE PROBLEMS Overwatering causes yellowing of the leaves.

■ CARE TIP

Natural trailing plants are ever popular for hanging containers, and this is one of them. Many are sold in plastic containers with snap-on base saucers which is fine for preventing drips when watering. But it is important to tip away any water that has gathered in the saucer following watering – the alternative is soggy soil and sick plants.

SCINDAPSUS

1.2m/4ft	60cm/24in	bright	10°C/50°F	high

The two types of scindapsus commonly available bear beautiful, glossy, heart-shaped leaves, sometimes marked silver or gold. They are climbers and need moss-covered supports to cling to.

GENERAL CARE Grow in a soil-based compost and water well during active growth. The plants like warmth but on very hot days will appreciate a misting over with water. Set in bright light, not direct sunlight, to maintain good leaf colour. Feed with liquid fertilizer every 2 weeks during the growth period. When the plant is resting, give it just enough water to prevent the compost from drying out. Repot annually in spring. When the plants have reached 20cm-8in pots, simply top-dress with fresh compost (*see p.14*).

PROPAGATION Take 10cm-4in tip cuttings in spring and root in equal parts peat and sand at 21-24°C/70-75°F. Plants raised from large-leaved cuttings will soon revert to producing small leaves.

VARIETIES *Scindapsus aureus* (*above left*), leaves a pointed oval when young, about 10cm/4in across, bright green marked yellow. Varieties include 'Golden Queen', almost completely yellow, and 'Marble Queen', white stems streaked green and cream leaves splashed with green and silver. *S. pictus argyraeus* (*above right*), matt green leaves spotted silver.

POSSIBLE PROBLEMS Overwatering causes leaves to yellow and fall.

▨ CARE TIP

The Devil's Ivy may also be seen with its more recent name of S. epipremnum, but whatever the name it is one of the best indoor plants for poor light locations, but needs to be warm and moist.

SCIRPUS

15cm/6in	25cm/6in	medium	7°C/45°F	high

Scirpus cernuus (*above*) is a member of the bulrush family, and, like its relative cyperus, likes to have its feet in water. The plant produces tufts of bright, slender green leaves from a creeping rootstock. So delicate are the leaves that they soon bend over the edge of the pot, making it almost impossible to place the plant anywhere else but in a hanging basket.

GENERAL CARE Grow in a soil-based compost kept constantly moist during the growing period. Water frequently – plants in hanging baskets dry out particularly quickly. Feeding is only necessary once every 4 weeks. Scirpus tolerate poor light well, for example at a north-facing window, but do not thrive in shade. During the resting period keep the compost just moist. Repot at any time if the surface of the compost becomes completely covered by the tufts of leaves. There are no named varieties.

PROPAGATION Divide overcrowded clumps in spring into 5cm/2in sections and replant immediately.

POSSIBLE PROBLEMS Generally trouble-free.

▨ DESIGN TIP

Something of a fun plant with its weeping slender tubes of growth – the sort of growth that one is often at a loss to know what should be done with the plant to make it more effective. One suggestion is to seek out a *ceramic head with a hole in the top rather than a mop of hair – the idea being that the scirpus placed in the hollow head becomes the flowing locks!*

SETCREASEA

| 38cm/15in | 60cm/24in | bright | 5°C/41°F | low |

Although setcreaseas bear tiny flowers in summer, it is for their extraordinary long pointed leaves that they are admired. In good light the foliage is a rich purple, contrasting well with the fresh green of the ubiquitous tradescantia, to which this plant is related. Setcreaseas are fast-growing and the trailing habit of growth can be rather untidy unless the shoots are regularly pinched out. There are no named varieties.

GENERAL CARE Grow in soil-based compost kept reasonably moist all year round, and feed with liquid fertilizer every 4 weeks. Good light is essential for leaf colour – several hours of direct sunlight every day is recommended. The ideal temperature is fairly warm, above 18°C/65°F. Repot whenever necessary; in practice setcreaseas are rarely kept beyond 2 years as they lose their good looks with age.

PROPAGATION Take 10cm/4in basal cuttings in summer.

POSSIBLE PROBLEMS Generally trouble-free.

SONERILA

| 15cm/6in | 20cm/8in | bright | 18°C/64°F | high |

Sonerila margaritacea is a low-growing, creeping plant with beautifully formed pointed leaves, green spotted silver, purple on the underside. The short stems are flushed with red. Tiny pink flowers appear in late summer. Because the plants grow continuously they are good subjects for closed containers or bottle gardens. For plants in room settings a short period of rest can be induced in the winter without doing any harm.

GENERAL CARE Grow in half-pots containing a peat-based compost to which a little leaf-mould, if available, has been added, with small pieces of crocks intermixed for improved drainage. Water moderately throughout the year. Sonerilas need good light, though not direct sunlight, and a warm atmosphere. Feed with liquid fertilizer every 2 weeks except for a brief period in winter if allowing the plants to rest. Repot annually in spring, and replace the plants when they become too leggy.

PROPAGATION Take 7.5cm/3in stem cuttings at any time except during a rest period. Set 3 cuttings to a 7.5cm/3in pot covered with a plastic bag until rooted, then gradually acclimatize them to normal conditions.

VARIETIES *S. m. hendersonii*, leaves more liberally spotted with white than the species; *S. m. argentea*, leaves almost completely silver; *S. m. marmorata*, leaves banded with silver.

POSSIBLE PROBLEMS Generally trouble-free.

■ DESIGN TIP

Often seen as pathetic single stems in pots that are too large. Overcome this problem by putting lots of cuttings in the pot at the outset and pinching out the tips once into growth.

■ CARE TIP

Not by any means the easiest of plants to manage, they are a bit like the fittonias that shrivel and die for little reason. As suggested for fittonias these would be much happier in the home if allowed the luxury of a large heated propagator in which to grow. A collection of these more tender plants with pots plunged in peat or moss can be a room feature.

TOLMIEA

| 15cm/6in | 30cm/12in | bright | 5°C/40°F | low |

Tolmiea menziesii is a member of the saxifrage family, and like *S. stolonifera* is sometimes called mother-of-thousands because of the way it freely produces its young. In this instance, however, the plantlets arise on the upper surface of the leaves, which explains tolmiea's more common name of 'piggy-back plant'. The leaves are slightly downy, shaped like a maple leaf, and the plants are nicely compact. There are no named varieties.

GENERAL CARE Grow in a soil-based compost. When in active growth water moderately and feed with liquid fertilizer every 2 weeks. Set in good light, out of direct sunlight. Tolmieas are accommodating as to temperature and fast-growing. repot at any time of year, but be prepared to replace old plants after a year or 18 months.

PROPAGATION Detach a leaf bearing a healthy plantlet and with a short length of stem. Place in trays or small pots of potting compost until rooted. Pot up 3 to a pot for the best effect.

POSSIBLE PROBLEMS generally trouble-free.

TRADESCANTIA

| 30cm/12in | 60cm/24in | bright | 10°C/50°F | low |

Tradescantias are the best-known trailing foliage plants, valued for their strong constitution and adaptabilty. The most popular varieties are those whose pointed oval leaves are variegated cream or white, but a green-leaved species is available. All look their best in hanging baskets or other situations where the trailing stems can fall freely.

GENERAL CARE Grow in soil-based compost kept reasonably moist during the active growing period. Feed with a liquid fertilizer every 2 weeks. Good light is important, though too much direct sunlight may scorch the leaves. Often these plants are kept at low temperatures, but they do best in warm rooms. Pinch out the growing tips to encourage bushy growth. Repot at any time of year, replacing old plants when they beome straggly.

PROPAGATION Take 10cm/4in tip cuttings at any time of year. Place in water, or place 6 cuttings in a 7.5cm/3in pot containing peat and sand until rooted and then pot up in the recommended compost.

SPECIES *Tradescantia fluminensis* 'Quicksilver' (*above*), strong-growing variety, prominent silver stripes; *T. blossfeldiana*, dark green leaves, purple beneath, in the variety 'Variegata' striped cream; *T. albiflora*, close growing species with many variegated forms, including 'Tricolor' with green leaves striped white and purple.

POSSIBLE PROBLEMS Overwatering reduces leaf colour.

■ GENERAL TIP

Most useful plants that are not only attractive indoors but also hardy in the garden – if less attractive owing to the effects of wind and rain. Outdoors offer sheltered location.

■ CARE TIP

Great favourites, these suffer from the old wives' advice of keeping them dry and unfed to preserve variegation in leaves. To maintain attractive colouring all poorly coloured foliage should be removed on sight and plants *should be fed and watered as one would any vigorous growing plant in a container. Five or six potfuls of cuttings in a hanging basket can be superb.*

YUCCA

1.8m/6ft	90cm/3ft	bright	7°C/45°F	low

The unusual yucca is a native of the south-east United States, and is commonly known as Spanish bayonet. At the top of a woody stem some 5cm/2in thick it bears a cluster of minutely toothed sword-shaped leaves. All forms of this eye-catching species are suited to a bright spacious entrance hall or porch.

GENERAL CARE Grow in a loam-based compost kept thoroughly moist during the growing period. Give a liquid feed every two weeks. Yuccas need bright light, including some direct sunlight, and are tolerant of a wide range of temperatures. They like a dry atmosphere. If possible, put them outside in a sunny spot for a few hours on summer days. Water sparingly in winter, and repot in spring if roots are overcrowded. Use heavy clay pots for stability.

PROPAGATION Professional growers cut the roots into 7.5cm/3in pieces and pot them up individually in sandy soil. This is difficult for amateurs, who do better to detach offsets, if they are produced, and treat them as cuttings.

SPECIES *P. aloifolia (above)*: blue-green leaves, stem normally unbranched except in the variety *P. a. draconis*: the leaves of *P. a. tricolor* have a central yellow stripe. *P. elephantipes*: several stems bearing glossy green leaves.

POSSIBLE PROBLEMS Leaf spot.

ZEBRINA

20cm/8in	60cm/24in	bright	10°C/50°F	low

Zebrina pendula belongs to the same family as tradescantias and has much the same habit of growth. It is quick-growing and will do better in cooler temperatures than tradescantias. There are some interesting coloured forms available; a mixed planting of different varieties looks very attractive, especially if trained upwards on thin stakes rather than left to trail freely.

GENERAL CARE Grow in soil-based compost and set several plants to each pot for a bushy effect. Pinch out the growing tips regularly. Water moderately while in active growth and feed with liquid fertilizer every 2 weeks. Place in good light in order to maintain leaf colour. A warm atmosphere is preferred. Repot whenever the roots become overcrowded.

PROPAGATION Take 7.5cm/3in tip cuttings in summer and treat as tradescantias.

VARIETIES *Z. p.* 'Discolor', slender leaves striped silver and bronze; 'Purpusii', large green leaves flushed purple, carmine beneath; 'Quadricolor', striped white, green and purple, purple beneath.

POSSIBLE PROBLEMS Leaves turn brown and fall in poor light or if overwatered.

▢ DESIGN TIP

Yuccas excel at the dramatic statement particularly in pairs flanking an archway or door. Especially effective when seen in silhouette, they look best against a plain, unpatterned background.

▢ GENERAL TIP

Often passed over as being too ordinary, the sparkling silver colouring of this plant is almost without equal. Select best colours when purchasing and remove all inferior foliage.

FLOWERING PLANTS

In purely practical terms, the main attraction of flowering houseplants is that they last so much longer than cut flowers. Indeed, some will be in bloom for months. Many are easy to care for, while others are a little fussier and give you an opportunity to practise your gardening skills. A bushy shape is common – with the notable exceptions of jasmine, clivia and columnea – but apart from this common feature there is an enormous variety of flower colour, leaf shape and overall size.

There is a flowering plant for every season. In winter, while the garden is almost bare of ornament, the house can be full of exuberant colour, with the pinks, purple and blues of cheerful cinerarias, bright yellow chrysanthemums, shocking pink cyclamens and vivid red poinsettias (*Euphorbia pulcherrima*). Jasmines, ruellias and the impressive strelitzias (not forgetting primulas and the contribution made by bulbs – see p. 78) bloom in spring. In summer the range of plants for indoor flowering is breathtaking. From the ever-popular fuchsia and fragrant Persian violet (*Exacum affine*) to the reliable buzy lizzie (impatiens) and exotic hoya, there is something to please all tastes and suit all situations.

SUCCESS WITH COLOUR

In terms of interior design foliage plants, including palms and ferns, have a certain versatility simply because they are, with some exceptions, uniformly green. While much of the charm of flowering plants naturally derives from the colour of their petals, to be displayed at their best some thought needs to be given to the overall colour scheme. In a room busy with patterns and prints, it is all too easy for plants to disappear against the background. In this situation, choose a plant whose flowers echo the brightest accent colour. The most effective is yellow, with vivid pink and red a close second and third. Draw attention to the plant with a careful choice of container; try a highly glazed pot in a plain colour complementing the flower, or a brass or copper pot with a burnished sheen. Display the pot against a plain wall which will act as a neutral background and, if painted in a pale shade, reflect some light back on the plant.

Modern room settings and offices tend to draw on a limited palette of subtle colours or simply stick to black and white. You can continue the understated feeling with a white cyclamen or hydrangea, especially in combination with sympathetic foliage plants; or use an unassertive colour scheme to set off plants that demand attention. Sinningias have it all: vivid, velvety trumpet-shaped flowers and huge dark green leaves. A collection of red or pink cinerarias looks stunning against white or cream. An orange clivia in full flower is like a piece of sculpture, perfect in light, spacious rooms.

PELARGONIUMS

Those fortunate enough to have sunny windows with deep sills have the ideal spot for a group of pelargoniums. The choice here is bewildering, and like roses and narcissi these are plants which have acquired a devoted following. As well as the zonal and regal types described on p. 59, there are species such as *P. crispum*, with balm-scented leaves, edged with creamy white in the variety 'Variegatum', and *P. tomentosum*, a climber with velvety leaves strongly scented with peppermint. These two species bear modest blooms of pink and white respectively. The best lemon-scented variety is 'Citriodorum'; 'Attar of Roses' is rose-scented. Both have pale mauve flowers. Pelargonium leaves vary in shape, colour and texture. Ivy-leaved forms are bright green and glossy; these are varieties of *P. peltatum*, a trailing species. They include the aristocratic

'L'Elegante', whose white flowers are feathered purple, the green leaves edged cream and flushed with purple as autumn approaches. *P. quercifolium*, the oak-leaved pelargonium, is at 90cm/3ft a good choice for conservatories and bears pink flowers veined with purple.

Pelargoniums are easy to raise from seed and can be successfully propagated by cuttings taken in summer. This method is also suitable for fuchsias, but it is advisable to leave more leaves on the cuttings. New plants may also be raised from overwintered specimens by taking cuttings in spring. Healthy but smaller plants are produced in this way.

PRIMULAS

Some types of flowering plants have been developed by plant breeders to flower at virtually any time of year in the extra warmth afforded to plants grown indoors. The most successful of these is the chrysanthemum, which is raised commercially in particular conditions. You can have your own primulas in bloom most of the year too, by choosing different varieties and sowing seed at different times. *P. malacoides* and *P. obconica* will produce large plants from seed sown in very early spring, but perfectly healthy specimens will result from sowings as late as midsummer, flowering correspondingly later. Sow seed as described on p. 14; for germination a temperature of 16°C/61°F is essential. Prick off the seedlings into boxes, then singly into 8cm/3½in pots. Spring-sown seedlings should be hardened off in an unheated frame during the summer. Transfer to the final pots in early autumn and bring indoors. They enjoy a cool spot indoors near a window to ensure constant light but without direct sunlight.

Primulas are available in a vast range of colours and can be grown from seed for winter and spring flowering.

ABUTILON

summer	1.2m/4ft	60cm/24in	bright	5°C/41°F

Abutilons are members of the mallow family, though because of the shape of the leaves they are often called flowering maples. There are several species suitable for indoor cultivation, but most need the space of a greenhouse. *A. × hybridum*, at 60cm/24in high (it is unlikely to reach the maximum height given above), is the most suitable for the home. It bears nodding flowers of white, yellow, orange or red from late spring right through to the autumn.

GENERAL CARE Grow in a soil-based compost kept nicely moist throughout the growing period. Feed with liquid fertilizer every 2 weeks and position the plants in an airy room where they will receive several hours of direct sunlight every day. During the rest period water enough to prevent the compost from drying out. Repot in spring, upgrading by one size. Plants grow spindly after 3 years and should be discarded.

PROPAGATION Take 10cm/4in tip cuttings in summer and root in equal parts peat and sand at a temperature of 15-18°C/59-64°F.

VARIETIES 'Master Hugh' (*above*), rich rose-pink; 'Boule de Neige', snow-white with golden stamens; 'Canary Bird' yellow.

POSSIBLE PROBLEMS Scale insects; mealy bugs.

ACALYPHA

summer	1.8m/6ft	90cm/3ft	bright	16°C/61°F

Known variously as the chenille plant or red hot cat's tail, *Acalypha hispida* is an exotic plant which can become very tall in a heated greenhouse. Even at 1.8m/6ft (the maximum height it will achieve in the home), it requires an unusual amount of space, which admirers of its spectacular flowers are happy to provide. These blooms are like catkins, up to 45cm/18in long and bright red. The vivid green leaves are pointed ovals up to 20cm/8in long.

GENERAL CARE Grow in a soil-based compost kept constantly moist during the growing season. Feed with liquid fertilizer every 2 weeks. Steady temperatures in the range 18-20°C/64-68°F or more are ideal, with humidity kept high with frequent mist-spraying. Stand the pots in trays of moist pebbles. Bright, filtered light is essential. Because acalyphas are naturally bushy, there is no need to pinch out the growing tips. Cutting back may, however, be necessary to restrict growth in confined areas. In winter, water just enough to keep the compost from drying out. Repot in spring, or at any other time if the roots are crowded. Discard after two seasons.

PROPAGATION Take 10cm/4in tip cuttings in early spring.

VARIETIES *A. h.* 'Alba', white-flowered type.

POSSIBLE PROBLEMS Red spider mite; mealy bug.

▤ PLANTING TIP

Only suitable if there is ample space for the amount of foliage that these plants are capable of producing. Over the summer months the problem can be side-stepped to some extent by planting plants as features in the garden. They can then be dug up, potted, trimmed back and re-introduced to a light and agreeable location indoors. Feed well when established.

▤ DESIGN TIP

In recent years often seen as a hanging plant in the Garden Centre, but it is far from happy in such elevated positions. Much better in large pots at ground level, by a pool perhaps.

Achimenes

| summer | 30cm/12in | 20cm/8in | bright | 2°C/35°F |

Once their simple requirements are met, these bushy plants produce their beautiful tubular flowers of crimson, red, lavender or purple right through the summer. The small, pointed leaves are dark green, sometimes flushed red.

GENERAL CARE Achimenes grow from small rhizomes. Plant in a peat-based compost to which a little ground limestone has been added to reduce acidity. Set 6 to a 12.5cm/5in pot or 8 to 15cm/6in pot and position where they will enjoy good light, but not direct sunlight. When growth starts in early spring, water copiously using cooled boiled water and never let the compost dry out. Start feeding with liquid fertilizer every 2 weeks when flowerbuds appear and continue until the flowers have faded. Spray plants with a fine mist on hot days. Support the stems with thin canes. After flowering, gradually reduce the amount of water until, in the dormant period, the pots are quite dry. Keep in a cool, frost-free place over winter. Repot in spring.

PROPAGATION When repotting, separate out the brittle rhizomes and pot up in the fresh compost. Place them horizontally just 1cm/½in below the surface of the compost.

SPECIES *Achimenes heterophylla*, orange flowers 4cm/½in wide; 'Little Beauty' (*above*) is a bushy variety with bright pink flowers; *A. grandiflora*, up to 60cm/24in high, erect plant with magenta flowers; *A. longiflora*, suitable for hanging baskets; set 10-12 rhizomes to a pot and stems will trail over the edge.

▇ CARE TIP

Bright and cheerful plants that are easy to manage on a light windowsill, but it is important to maintain good and steady temperature during the early weeks of development. The obscure common name of Hot Water Plant is difficult to reason with, but may allude to watering with warm water following winter rest.

Anthurium

| spring | 23cm/9in | 23cm/9in | medium | 10°C/50°F |

Anthuriums are natives of South America, where they grow to massive proportions. As house plants, however, they are compact but bushy. The best flowering species is *A. scherzerianum*, the flamingo flower, which is spectacularly colourful from spring right through to mid autumn. Its inflorescences consist of a large scarlet spathe from which a narrow, curly orange spadix emerges. They may need the support of thin canes. The pointed dark green leaves, up to 15cm/6in long, are equally handsome. There are no named varieties.

GENERAL CARE Grow in a fibrous open mixture consisting of fibrous peat, sphagnum moss, crushed charcoal and a little soil-based compost, with a generous layer of drainage material at the bottom of the pot. Plants should not be set too deep. Keep the compost thoroughly moist but not waterlogged during the growing period and feed with liquid fertilizer every 2 weeks. Success depends on steadily maintained temperatures between 18 and 21°C/64 and 70°F – draughts spell disaster – and high humidity. Stand the pots on trays of moist pebbles and spray the foliage with a fine mist daily. It helps to position anthuriums in groups of other plants, where humidity is usually higher. Place in slight shade. In winter, keep the compost just moist. Repot in spring, upgrading by one size.

PROPAGATION Divide the roots in early spring.

POSSIBLE PROBLEMS Aphids; leaf spot.

▇ GENERAL TIP

Besides A. schertzerianum there is the more exotic and more demanding A. andreanum which has bold arrow-shaped leaves and spathe inflorescences in various colours on metre-long stems. Blooms are much in demand by the keen flower arranger and they have long-lasting qualities when cut that make them doubly useful. Generous warmth and moist surroundings are essential.

APHELANDRA

summer	30cm/12in	25cm/10in	bright	13°C/55°F

Only one species of aphelandra, *A. squarrosa*, is grown as a house plant and while its vivid yellow flowers are showy enough, the foliage is equally eye-catching. The broad green leaves are up to 30cm/12in long, veined in a sharply contrasting cream, hence the popular name of zebra plant.

GENERAL CARE Grow in a peat-based compost kept constantly moist during the growing season. Feed with liquid fertilizer once a week and keep at a steady temperature of about 18°C/64°F. High humidity is important – stand the pots in saucers of moist pebbles and mist over with a very fine spray every few days. The plants need good but indirect light. In the brief winter rest period, water just enough to prevent the stems from drooping. After flowering, cut back the main stem to a healthy pair of leaves. This will encourage the production of side shoots for propagation. Repot in spring, upgrading to a final pot size of 15cm/6in.

PROPAGATION Detach side shoots when 10cm/4in long and use as cuttings. Root in equal parts of peat and sand at 21°C/70°F.

VARIETIES *A. s.* 'Louisae' (*above*), orange-yellow bracts, red stems; 'Leopoldii', red bracts, pure white leaf markings; 'Citrina', sharp yellow bracts.

POSSIBLE PROBLEMS Aphids, scale insects and mealy bugs on young growths.

▨ PROPAGATION TIP

Keeping these from year to year is seldom successful indoors – much better to have a propagator and to raise cuttings made from shoots that form in the leaf axils of older plants.

AZALEA

winter	60cm/24in	60cm/24in	moderate	7°C/45°F

The pot plants sold in winter by florists as Indian azaleas are varieties of *Rhododendron simsii*, a Chinese species. Sometimes they are (wrongly) labelled *R. indicum*, which confusingly enough comes from Japan and is an evergreen that may reach 1.8m/6ft. *R. simsii* can reach 1.5m/6ft in a sheltered garden but is more compact grown in pots. Its gorgeous winter display of exotic blooms in a wide range of colours (except blue) has made the azalea very popular.

GENERAL CARE Choose a specimen just coming into bud. Place in a cool situation protected from draughts and keep moist by immersing the pot in water 2-3 times a week for 5 minutes. Always use rainwater or cooled boiled water. Do not feed. After flowering keep very cool and just moist. Place outside in a shaded position after all danger of frost has passed. Keep shaded and moist, spraying frequently, until bringing indoors again as winter begins. Repot in autumn using an acid compost.

PROPAGATION Take 7.5cm/3in cuttings in summer and root them in a mixture of 2 parts fine sand and 1 part peat. When rooted pot in compost of peat, leaf-mould, lime-free loam and coarse sand in equal proportions.

VARIETIES Florists' azaleas are unlikely to be named.

POSSIBLE PROBLEMS Lime in the water or growing medium will invariably result in yellow foliage, poor growth and ultimate collapse.

▨ CARE TIP

The period following flowering is a critical time for these plants – often the time for most neglect. Remove dead flowers carefully so that new growth buds below the flowers are not damaged, and keep the plant moist and protected from frost until it is safe to put it outside in a lightly shaded, sheltered location. Keep watered and fed while outside – bring in before frosts occur.

BEGONIA SEMPERFLORENS

spring	23cm/9in	23cm/9in	bright	13°C/55°F

Wax begonias, *Begonia semperflorens-cultorum*, bear their small but brilliantly coloured flowers all summer if grown outdoors. If you select F_1 hybrids, however, and grow them on a sunny windowsill indoors, they are almost perpetual flowering. Blooms are white and shades of pink or red; the foliage may be dark red or brown or green.

GENERAL CARE Grow in a peat-based compost kept moist but not waterlogged. Feed with liquid fertilizer every 2 weeks. Set the pots in good light, preferably where the plants can enjoy a few hours of direct sunlight every day. Normal room temperatures are suitable. Discard the plants after flowering.

PROPAGATION *B. semperflorens* are fibrous-rooted begonias, raised from seed. Sow seed in very early spring at 16°C/61°F. Plants should be ready for final potting up in about 10 weeks.

VARIETIES Red/brown leaves: 'Carmen', pink; 'Comet' (F_1), all colours; 'Coffee and Cream', white. Green leaves: 'Bella', rich pink; 'Scarletta', deep red; 'Organdy Mixture' (F_1), all colours.

POSSIBLE PROBLEMS Generally trouble-free.

▇ PLANTING TIP

Before frosts arrive dig up some of these from the garden and pot into containers for the summer display to continue on the windowsill indoors until the following spring – perhaps longer!

BEGONIA TUBERHYBRIDA

summer	45cm/18in	20cm/8in	bright	5°C/41°F

The flowers of tuberous begonias, *Begonia tuberhybrida*, are among the most flamboyant of all house plants. Double-flowered varieties are available, as well as types with pendulous blooms, ideal for hanging baskets.

GENERAL CARE Buy tubers in spring and place concave side up in trays of damp seed compost. Set them 5cm/2in apart and press down to half their depth. Position on a warm windowsill and when 2-3 leaves have opened up, pot up in a peat-based mixture so that the tuber is just visible. Place in light shade, gradually pot on and bring into bright but filtered light. Water moderately during the flowering period and give a high-potassium liquid feed every 2 weeks. To allow the showy male flowers to develop, remove the small female flowers when they appear. In winter, let the compost dry out place in a frost-free place or remove the tubers and store them in clean dry sand over winter.

PROPAGATION In spring, cut large tubers into sections, each with a growing point, and treat as above.

VARIETIES Double: 'Buttermilk', cream; 'Crown Prince', crimson; 'Everest', white, frilled petals; 'Midas' golden yellow; 'Ninette', pale apricot, very large; 'Rebecca', light pink, blooms like rosebuds. *B. t. pendula* (trailing stems): 'Yellow Sweetie', scented; 'Roberta', scarlet.

POSSIBLE PROBLEMS Weevils, eelworms; grey mould.

▇ GENERAL TIP

To see these at their best visit the British Begonia Championships – you may well not believe what your eyes are feasting on. But it must be said that such plants are grown from expensive named varieties. To do well all tuberous begonias should be started in late winter in almost dry peat and thereafter given little water until growth is evident.

BELOPERONE

spring	60cm/24in	45cm/18in	medium	7°C/45°F

Only one species of beloperone, a native of Mexico, is in general cultivation. *B. guttata* is commonly known as the shrimp plant because of the appearance of its inflorescences, pinkish bracts surrounding insignificant flowers. These hang on arching stems and are borne profusely from spring until the middle of winter. With its light green pointed leaves and bushy habit, the shrimp plant is very decorative. Provide thin stakes to support mature plants. There are no named varieties.

GENERAL CARE Grow in a rich, soil-based compost and keep well watered throughout the growing period. Strong sunlight will scorch the flowers, but reasonably bright light is best as long as the plants are in a well-ventilated room (as opposed to a draughty corner) and are not allowed to dry out. Temperatures of about 15°C/59°F will encourage long-lasting flowers. Feed with a liquid fertilizer once a week from the time flowering starts until autumn. Reduce watering during the winter, giving just enough to prevent the compost drying out. In early spring, cut back the plant to keep it bushy, and repot if necessary, adding a little peat to the compost.

PROPAGATION Take 7.5cm/3in stem cuttings in spring and root in a mixture of peat and sand at 18°C/64°F.

POSSIBLE PROBLEMS Generally trouble-free.

BROWALLIA

summer	45cm/18in	25cm/10in	bright	10°C/50°F

Browallias are annual plants grown for their display of vivid purplish-blue five-petalled flowers. Two species are available, bearing blooms in summer or winter depending on the time of sowing. The slender stems may need the support of thin stakes, or can be left to trail over the edge of the pot if displayed in hanging baskets.

GENERAL CARE Grow in 12.5cm/5in pots containing a soil-based mixture. Water moderately, allowing the compost to dry out a little between applications. Feed established plants with liquid fertilizer every 2 weeks. Browallias thrive in good light, including several hours of direct sunlight every day, but keep temperatures below 18°C/64°F to encourage long-lasting flowers. The ideal temperature is given above. Pinch out the growing tips regularly to encourage a bushy shape. Discard the plants after flowering.

PROPAGATION Sow seed in spring for late summer flowering, in late summer for a winter display.

SPECIES *B. speciosa* (*above*), 5cm/2in wide flowers in bloom for 4 months; *B. s. major* is the best variety for winter-flowering; 'Silver Bells' is a white-flowered form. *B. viscosa* is more compact at 30cm/12in, with smaller flowers.

POSSIBLE PROBLEMS Generally trouble-free.

■ CARE TIP

Much underrated plants on account of their need for frequent feeding and regular potting on. Both these actions will produce much more lush plants with infinitely more flowering bracts.

■ PROPAGATION TIP

Many of the seed-raised house plants are the prerogative of the commercial grower with ideal conditions at his disposal, but there are numerous kinds that can be raised on the windowsill indoors and this is one of them.

Sow lightly in shallow seed trays filled with peat and sand mixture and cover with a sheet of glass until seed has germinated. Protect with paper from sun.

CALCEOLARIA

| spring | 45cm/18in | 30cm/12in | bright | 10°C/50°F |

The calceolaria family includes hundreds of species, including some alpines, but only one is in general use as a flowering house plant. This is the hybrid *Calceolaria herbeohybrida*, and although its flowering period is brief it is dazzlingly colourful. The slipper-shaped flowers, clustering above large, oval, slightly hairy leaves, are orange, yellow or red and often blotched with a contrasting colour. A dwarf strain with particularly attractive blooms is also available.

GENERAL CARE Grow in a mixture of soil-based compost and peat – calceoloarias like a slightly acid soil. Keep the compost constantly and evenly moist. It is a good idea to stand the pots in trays of moist peat to keep the humidity level high. While the flowering period (at best about a month) can be extended by keeping the plants cool, it is equally important to give them bright light, though not direct sunlight. Feeding is not necessary and the plants should be discarded after flowering.

PROPAGATION Calceolarias are raised commercially in great numbers and are widely available. If you wish to raise your own, sow the tiny seeds in summer. Overwinter the seedlings at 7-10°C/45-50°F before final potting up.

VARIETIES *C. h.* 'Monarch', a reliable strain which includes mixed colours; 'Multiflora Nana', up to 20cm/8in high, with abundant flowers.

POSSIBLE PROBLEMS Aphids.

■ CARE TIP

These should be watered with care avoiding getting water onto the foliage of the plants. Ideally, the leaves should be lifted while water is carefully poured onto the soil surface.

CAMPANULA

| summer | 15cm/6in | 45cm/18in | bright | 4.5°C/40°F |

The bell-flower family includes a huge variety of plants, one of which has become popular for indoor decoration. This is *Campanula isophylla*, native to northern Italy, a perennial which can successfully be grown outdoors in favoured districts. Low-growing, its long stems may be trained up thin stakes or left to trail gracefully over the side of the pot, especially if displayed in a hanging basket. Star-shaped pale lilac flowers appear in mid summer and persist for up to 12 weeks, becoming so numerous that the tangled, heart-shaped leaves are almost completely concealed.

GENERAL CARE Grow in soil-based compost kept well-watered though never waterlogged. Even in the rest period campanulas like their roots nicely damp. Feed with liquid fertilizer every 2 weeks until flowering is over. Keep cool during flowering, while ensuring bright light at all times. Spray with a fine mist to maintain humidity, especially if the temperature rises above 18°C/64°F. Deadhead regularly, and before the rest period cut all stems right back. Repot in early spring if necessary.

PROPAGATION Take 5cm/2in tip cuttings in early spring, ensuring that each has 4 pairs of leaves.

VARIETIES *C. a.* 'Alba' (above), white-flowered form; 'Mayi', blue flowers, variegated leaves.

POSSIBLE PROBLEMS Generally trouble-free.

■ FLOWERING TIP

There are blue and white flowered forms and, though seen less often, the white form makes a much bolder and more attractive plant. In hanging containers in a cool room or conservatory they will flower for months on end during the spring and summer. But it is vital that dead flowers be removed almost continuously to prevent formation of seed and an end of flowers.

CAPSICUM

summer	38cm/15in	38cm/15in	bright	7°C/45°F

The ornamental pepper, *Capsicum annum*, belongs to the same family as edible peppers; in theory the fruits of this species are edible too, but bearing in mind the fact that the smallest peppers are the hottest, these are likely to be unbearably fiery. Decorative they certainly are, in a range of colours including red, orange, yellow and purple, all of which are green, then creamy-yellow, when young. They last for weeks. The leaves are pointed and the whole plant attractively bushy.

GENERAL CARE Most capsicums are bought with the fruit already formed. Choose a compact, bushy plant with green (young) fruits. Keep at normal room temperatures – cooler if possible – and make sure that the compost is always thoroughly moist. Feed with liquid fertilizer every 2 weeks. Bright light is essential, including several hours of direct sunlight every day. The fruits stay colourful and plump for up to 12 weeks, but eventually shrivel and fall, at which point the plant should be discarded.

PROPAGATION Raising capsicums from seed is beyond the scope of most amateurs.

VARIETIES There are several named varieties, but the great majority on sale will be anonymous, even if of excellent quality.

POSSIBLE PROBLEMS Aphids, red spider mites.

CHRYSANTHEMUM

all year	23cm/9in	20cm/8in	moderate	2°C/36°F

There are an enormous number of garden chrysanthemums of different kinds and sizes. A few of these have been selected for special treatment to keep the growth compact (in the garden chrysanthemums can reach 1.2m/4ft in height) and to permit flowering at any time of year. The colour range of these attractively bushy specimens includes white, yellow, red, pink and bronze.

GENERAL CARE Buy chrysanthemums with a few flowers opening, the rest still in green buds just flushed with colour. Keep well watered, in reasonable light and as cool as possible to encourage a long flowering period. In favourable conditions plants can be expected to last up to 8 weeks. Remove flowers as they fade. Neither feeding nor repotting is necessary and after flowering these plants should be discarded.

PROPAGATION It is not possible for amateurs to raise chrysanthemums under the artificial conditions necessary to produce these compact plants.

VARIETIES Chrysanthemums sold as pot plants do not usually bear a particular name.

POSSIBLE PROBLEMS Generally trouble-free.

▨ CARE TIP

Hot, dry atmosphere will increase incidence of pests – aphids and red spider mites. To counteract both it is wise to treat plants with a systemic insecticide before pests appear.

▨ CARE TIP

For their 6/8 week flowering life indoors these are foolproof plants if offered cool, light and reasonably moist conditions. Growers treat with growth retardants to control height.

CINERARIA

| winter | 38cm/15in | 38cm/15in | moderate | 7°C/45°F |

Although correctly named *Senecio cruentus*, these colourful, winter- and spring-flowering pot plants are always known as cinerarias. They produce masses of daisy-like flowers of pink, purple, red or blue, sometimes zoned with white. The compact mound of blooms is framed by large, dark green palmate leaves. Different strains have been developed, including dwarf varieties.

GENERAL CARE Cinerarias are available as pot plants from the late autumn. Buy specimens whose buds are just beginnning to show colour. Kept cool, moist and shaded, the plants will last up to 7 weeks. Water regularly as cinerarias lose moisture quickly through their large leaves. Feeding is not necessary. Discard the plants after flowering.

PROPAGATION Sow seeds in early summer for a mid-winter flowering, 4 weeks later for a spring flowering. Feed the young plants once a week in the autumn (before they come into flower) with half-strength liquid fertilizer.

VARIETIES Hybrida Grandiflora strain; 'Brilliant', up to 53cm/21in high with large flowers; Double-flowered strain: 'Gubler's Double Mixed', about 38cm/15in high with double or semi-double flowers; Multiflora Nana strain: 'Gem Mixed', about 30cm/12in high, broad-petalled flowers.

POSSIBLE PROBLEMS Aphids; leaf miners.

■ CARE TIP

To prolong flowering period indoors it is essential to offer these plants cool, airy and light conditions – in warm rooms, added to the shorter flowering life, there will also be a much greater incidence of pests. And these plants when in weak condition through improper care will attract all the pests in the book. Frequent inspection of undersides of leaves is needed.

CLIVIA

| spring | 60cm/24in | 30cm/12in | bright | 10°C/50°F |

The kaffir lily, *Clivia miniata*, is a spectacular flowering plant from South Africa. It produces several straight flower-bearing stalks from a bulbous base of overlapping leaves. The trumpet-shaped blooms of orange or yellow appear in abundant clusters. There are no named varieties.

GENERAL CARE Plant crowns when they become available in early spring, setting them in 12.5cm/5in pots of soil-based compost. Put in a position where they will enjoy good direct light, but out of the midday sun. Clivias thrive in average room temperature. Keep well watered during the spring and summer and start to feed with liquid fertilizer when the flower stalks are about 20cm/8in high. As autumn approaches, cease feeding and gradually decrease the amount of water leading up to a revitalizing rest period in early winter. During this time the compost should be almost dry and the temperature cool. Protect from frost. Repot after 2-3 years, after flowering, when the roots – which grow quickly – have filled the pot. Once plants have reached a 25cm/10in pot, simply top-dress annually (*see page 14*).

PROPAGATION Separate old plants into crowns, taking care not to damage the roots, and pot up singly. Clivias produce offsets which can happily be left on the plant, but if wished can be detached with a sharp knife and potted up. Do this after flowering, selecting offsets with at least 3 good leaves.

POSSIBLE PROBLEMS Mealy bugs.

■ FLOWERING TIP

Extremely resilient plants in reasonable conditions, but not easy to bring into flower. Like many native South African plants they need a dry resting period to encourage flowering. Alternatively, if a heated conservatory is available they can be planted in a bed of good soil where they will produce an abundance of their rich, orange-coloured flowers.

COLUMNEA

| winter | 90cm/3ft | 90cm/3ft | bright | 13°C/55°F |

There are several species of columneas used as house plants; they are pendulous plants best seen in hanging baskets. Yellow or red flowers appear over many weeks in winter or spring.

GENERAL CARE Grow in a mixture of 2 parts peat-crushed compost and 1 part sphagnum moss, adding a little crushed charcoal to improve aeration. Keep the compost constantly moist, and mist the plants over with a spray of rainwater as often as possible. In summer, give a liquid feed at half-strength every week. Hang the baskets in full light, out of direct sun, and maintain a steady temperature of around 16°C/61°F in winter if possible. Pinch the stems back to encourage a bushy shape and cut them right back after flowering. Repot every other year.

PROPAGATION Take 7.5 cm/3in cuttings of non-flowering stems in spring and root in a mixture of equal parts peat and sand at 18-21°C/64-70°F. Pot up when established, setting 3 plants to a 25cm/10in basket.

VARIETIES *Columnea × banksii*, flowering winter into spring, orange-red blooms, glossy leaves; *C. gloriosa*, abundant scarlet flowers, splashed yellow, in winter, pale green leaves; *C. microphylla*, winter flowering, orange flowers, trailing stems up to 1.8m/6ft; *C. 'Alpha' (above)*, hybrid bearing clear yellow flowers all year; *C. 'Mary Ann'*, deep pink flowers all year.

POSSIBLE PROBLEMS Generally trouble-free if high levels of humidity are maintained.

▣ FLOWERING TIP

Some easy, some difficult, but all will flower more freely if they have a slightly drier and a cooler period prior to their normal flowering time, which may be winter or summer.

CYCLAMEN

| autumn/winter | 45cm/18in | 30cm/12in | moderate | 7°C/45°F |

Cyclamens developed from *Cyclamen persicum* are one of the most popular flowering house plants, bearing butterfly-shaped flowers of white, pink or red on straight stems rising from a cluster of heart-shaped mid-green leaves, often beautifully marked with silver. They require particular conditions to do well, and are rarely worth keeping for a second year.

GENERAL CARE Cyclamens are available from the autumn, potted up in a peat-based compost with half the corm visible above the surface. Choose a plant in bud; well-cared-for, it will be in flower for up to 3 months. Do not subject cyclamens to drastic changes in temperature. They like to be cool, ideally at 13°C/55°F; up to 18°C/64°F is acceptable with increased humidity, but any warmer and the plant will certainly suffer. Water daily by placing the pot in a plant saucer filled with water and leave to stand for 10 minutes. The plant will take up enough water for its needs. Water from above only if you have a steady hand and can be sure of not wetting the corm, which is subject to rot. Give a liquid feed every 2 weeks. Stand in good light, not direct sunlight. Remove faded flowers and discoloured leaves.

PROPAGATION Cyclamens can only be raised from seed.

VARIETIES 'Perfection Mixed', red, pink, magenta, white; 'Rex', all colours, leaves splashed silver; 'Ruffled Hybrids', all colours, fringed petals.

POSSIBLE PROBLEMS Grey mould.

▣ CARE TIP

The modern, quickly-grown, F₁ (first selection seed) cyclamen are brought from seed sowing to flowering in some eight months, but they seem much softer than the older style plant – perhaps the price of progress. Plants with large and firm corms can be kept from one year to the next by drying them off and storing in a cool, dry place until growth appears in new season.

EUPHORBIA

| winter | 1.2m/4ft | 38cm/15in | bright | 13°C/55°F |

Euphorbias are a huge family of plants, one of which is extremely popular as a decorative house plant. This is *Euphorbia pulcherrima*, the species universally known as poinsettia. The Latin suffix means 'most beautiful'. The true flowers are insignificant, all the colour deriving from showy bracts which are usually scarlet but may be pink or cream. These plants are commercially produced under special conditions which delay their development and inhibit their natural growth to make them compact enough for use in the home. The milky sap is poisonous.

GENERAL CARE Keep newly purchased plants at a moderate, steady temperature, preferably with other plants so that humidity is reasonably high. Place the plant in good light, such as sunlight filtered through a fine curtain. Water when the foliage begins to droop, and then give the plant plenty to drink, without allowing it to become waterlogged. No feeding is required. Discard the plant after flowering.

PROPAGATION Raising poinsettias is not recommended for the amateur.

VARIETIES Most commercially raised poinsettias do not bear names.

POSSIBLE PROBLEMS Generally trouble-free.

◼ GENERAL TIP

These can easily attain 2m (6ft) height when grown in pots, but to ensure short plants of compact appearance the grower treats his plants with a growth retarding chemical – a professional task.

EXACUM

| summer | 23cm/9in | 15cm/6in | bright | 10°C/50°F |

Known as the Persian violet, *Exacum affine* (*above*) is in fact a member of the gentian family. Neat and bushy, its purple flowers, with prominent yellow centres, appear throughout the summer, cushioned by a mass of shiny, oval leaves. Some recently developed strains are fragrant, as is the species.

GENERAL CARE Buy plants that are just coming into flower, and keep them in a reasonably warm room protected from sudden changes in temperature. Keep the compost constantly and thoroughly moist and set the pots in saucers of moist pebbles to keep the level of humidity high. It also helps to keep several pots together (and they look particularly attractive in groups). While the plants are in flower, feed every 2 weeks with liquid fertilizer and remove faded flowers to prolong the flowering period. Set the pots in good light but not in direct sunlight. Discard plants after flowering.

PROPAGATION Exacums can be raised from seed sown in spring. Set the seedlings 5 to a 10cm/4in pot for the best effect. use a compost of equal parts peat and loam, with a little fine sand to assist drainage.

VARIETIES *E. a.* 'Starlight Fragrance', a reliable strain with spicy scent.

POSSIBLE PROBLEMS Generally trouble-free.

◼ GENERAL TIP

Neat and attractive windowsill plants that are reasonably easy to raise from seed. Alas, the average householders often feel that this is beyond them, but it is perfectly possible to sow and bring on young plants on a bright *bedroom windowsill indoors – it is not necessary to have a greenhouse and attendant facilities for simple plants of this kind.*

FUCHSIA

| summer | 60cm/24in | 60cm/24in | bright | 4.5°C/40°F |

Fuchsias include literally hundreds of garden varieties, some hardy, some tender, and numerous perennial species which are suitable for the cool greenhouse – and, therefore, certain indoor situations. Their blooms are unique: pendulous, consisting of a bell-shaped flower (often purple) surrounded by 4 sepals (often bright pink).

GENERAL CARE Grow in a soil-based compost kept nicely moist during the flowering period. Feed with liquid fertilizer once a week as the buds are forming. Pinch out the growing tip to encourage bushy growth. Set in good light, not direct sunlight. Choose a cool, well-ventilated (not draughty) place where the temperature is steady. After flowering, reduce the amount of water and cut back to strong stems. Overwinter in a frost-free place, keeping the compost just moist. In spring, when new shoots appear, cut back to form a strong stem system.

PROPAGATION Take 10cm/4in tip cuttings in autumn or spring and insert singly in 5cm/2in pots containing equal parts of sand and peat at a temperature of 16°C/61°F.

VARIETIES 'Cascade', white sepals streaked pink, crimson petals; 'Falling Stars', red sepals, deep red petals; 'Golden Marinka', red flowers, golden yellow leaves; 'Swingtime', red sepals, white double petals; 'Thalia' (*above*), long, red flowers.

POSSIBLE PROBLEMS Aphids; whitefly.

▓ CARE TIP

These often shed flowers alarmingly when brought indoors – to counteract, choose plants in bud, not in flower, and offer them the lightest and coolest window location in the room.

HIBISCUS

| summer | 38cm/15in | 38cm/15in | bright | 7°C/45°F |

The rose of China, *Hibiscus rosa-sinensis* (*above*), can reach 1.8m/6ft in the wild. It is much more compact when grown in pots, and produces a succession of beautiful 12.5cm/5in wide flowers of white, red, orange, pink or yellow throughout the summer. The broad, pointed leaves are dark green and glossy.

GENERAL CARE Grow in a rich, soil-based compost kept evenly moist throughout the flowering period and give a liquid feed every 2 weeks. Bright light is important, including a few hours of direct sunlight every day. Normal room temperatures are suitable until flowering is over; during the rest period keep the plants cool and barely moist, and cease feeding. In spring the following year, cut back all growth to 15cm/6in after repotting into a pot one size larger.

PROPAGATION Take 10cm/4in tip cuttings in spring and root in a potting mixture of equal parts peat and sand at 18°C/64°F.

VARIETIES Hibiscus plants sold as house plants are generally unnamed, though they are reliable if bought from a reliable source. Look out for the variety *H. r.* 'Cooperi', with leaves variegated cream flushed red.

POSSIBLE PROBLEMS Aphids; mealy bugs.

▓ CARE TIP

These are plants that can attain considerable age even when roots are confined to pots. Given time and care a main stem can be tied to a support so that it attains a height of 1m (3ft) or more, at which point the tip can be removed to encourage the plant to branch. The effect will be similar to that of a standard fuchsia with trumpet flowers set off to considerable advantage.

HOYA

summer	30cm/12in	38cm/15in	bright	10°C/50°F

There are two species of hoya in general use. *Hoya carnosa*, the wax plant, is a climber reaching 5m/16ft and needs the space of a conservatory. More suitable for the average room is the diminutive *H. bella* (*above*), from India, which bears trusses of sweetly scented white or pink flowers all the summer.

GENERAL CARE Grow in peat-based compost kept nicely moist throughout the growing period. Set the plants in good light; an hour or two of direct sunlight every day will do no harm. Feed occasionally with liquid fertilizer – if the plant is becoming leafy with few flowers, dilute the feed and lengthen the intervals between applications. *H. bella* likes a warm room and high humidity; spray the leaves daily with rainwater or cooled boiled water before the flowers have opened. After flowering the faded blooms should be removed with extreme care, as the new flower is forming on the spur behind it. These buds can easily fall off if disturbed – so do not move the pot once you can see them. Keep the compost barely moist during the winter, but continue to give the plants full light. Repot every other spring, upgrading one size.

PROPAGATION Take 7.5cm/3in cuttings in early summer and root in equal parts sand and peat at a temperature of 16-18°C/61-64°F.

POSSIBLE PROBLEMS Overwatering, or the use of hard water, will turn the leaves brown.

▨ FLOWERING TIP

Getting these to flower can be a problem – to encourage keep dry in cool window over the winter and, when into growth for the new season, feed with a tomato fertilizer.

HYDRANGEA

spring	60cm/24in	60cm/24in	bright	13°C/55°F

Potted hydrangeas, varieties of the garden species *Hydrangea macrophylla*, are available in spring and bloom indoors for several weeks before being discarded (or planted outside). They are beautiful specimens for a table display. Flower colour is blue, white or pink.

GENERAL CARE Blue-flowered hydrangeas must be grown in an acid medium to retain their colour; the pink-flowered kinds need an alkaline medium. In the wrong potting mixture blues will turn purplish-pink and pinks turn blue-purple. Keep the plants cool to prolong flowering and in bright light, not direct sunlight. Do not allow the compost to dry out at any time. Submerging the pot in water for a few minutes each day is a good way to ensure constant moisture. Give a feed of liquid fertilizer every 2 weeks during flowering. Repotting is not necessary. After flowering either discard the plants or set them outside in a sheltered spot (remembering the effects of acid/alkaline soil on flower colour).

PROPAGATION Raising hydrangeas for pot culture is not recommended for amateurs.

VARIETIES Most varieties on offer are forms of *H. m.* 'Hortensia' (*above*) although lacecap types are sometimes available.

POSSIBLE PROBLEMS Aphids.

▨ DESIGN TIP

Naturally pink coloured, hydrangeas can be changed to blue (albeit, often a washed-out colour) by adding alum or a proprietary colourant to the soil. Following flowering indoors plants can be potted into tubs or large pots to become attractive features on the patio in subsequent years.

IMPATIENS

summer	23cm/9in	30cm/12in	bright	13°C/55°F

A healthy specimen of impatiens, though spreading, is neat and compact. The leaves should be bright green and the whole plant covered in vivid flowers of red, pink or white from spring to autumn.

GENERAL CARE Grow in 12.5cm/5in pots of good soil-based compost kept moderately watered throughout the flowering season. Feed occasionally with a solution of Epsom salts (1 teaspoon to 600 ml/1 pint of water) to maintain good leaf colour. Mist over the plants regularly with a fine spray. Set them in good light, avoiding direct sunlight, in normal room temperatures. Pinch out the growing tips regularly or the plants become straggly. Overwinter at the recommended temperature, keeping the compost just moist.

PROPAGATION Raise hybrids from seed, named varieties of species from 10cm/4in cuttings taken at any time between spring and autumn and root in equal parts sand and peat at a temperature of 16°C/61°F.

VARIETIES *Impatiens holstii* (syn. *I. walleriana*), bushy, short-lived perennial, bright scarlet flowers; *I. petersiana*, up to 90cm/3ft high and needing support, bronze-red foliage, deep pink flowers. Hybrids include the Imp strain (*above*); flowers white, orange, scarlet, pink, red and purple; 'Fantastic Rose' (*above*), 'Orange Baby'; 'Scarlet Baby'.

POSSIBLE PROBLEMS Aphids; red spider mite.

▓ CARE TIP

The New Guinea hybrid impatiens make an interesting change and have colourful foliage to add to their list of features. These must be kept wet, regularly fed and potted into rich compost.

JASMINUM

winter/spring	3m/10ft	30cm/12in	bright	7°C/45°F

Delightful as they are, jasmines do not have a long life as house plants because they are such rampant growers that eventually a home has to be found for them elsewhere, in a conservatory or garden room. The most popular indoor species, *Jasminum polyanthum*, is a native of China, and bears abundant, heavily scented white tubular flowers in winter and spring. There are no named varieties.

GENERAL CARE Jasmines are often sold trained around a hoop, but they will soon need further support from canes or thin stakes. keep the plants cool, in the best light available, and water frequently, using tepid water, without allowing the compost to become waterlogged. Feed every 2 weeks with liquid fertilizer while in active growth. Pot on in the summer, upgrading one size and using a soil-based compost. The larger the pot, the greater the possible height of the plant; be aware that it may eventually outgrow the space you have available. Cut back hard after flowering. During the rest period keep the compost just moist.

PROPAGATION Take 10cm/4in tip cuttings in summer or early autumn and root in equal parts sand and peat at a temperature of 16°C/61°F.

POSSIBLE PROBLEMS Red spider mite.

▓ CARE TIP

The skills of the commercial grower of these plants has made it possible for him to produce neat plants of about 1m (6ft) tall and full of flowers during the winter months when plants are normally purchased. Following flowering, the plant tends to grow apace needing a frame for its growth. Subsequent flowering is often difficult, but dry autumn conditions will help.

KOHLERIA

summer	60cm/24in	30cm/12in	bright	12°C/54°F

Kohlerias come from South America, and need some of the warmth and humidity of their native habitat to succeed. Given congenial conditions, they produce beautiful bell-shaped flowers of pink or red throughout the summer; indeed, by taking cuttings at intervals you can have them in flower all year round.

GENERAL CARE Kohlerias grow from rhizomes. In very early spring, place rhizomes just below the surface in shallow trays of peat at 21°C/70°F. Pot them up when growth has reached 5cm/2in, placing 3 to a 12.5cm/5in pot containing a peat-based compost. Keep moderately moist until the plants are well established, then reduce the temperature to 18°C/64°F and increase the amount of water. Kohlerias like bright light, including direct sunlight; give protection from fierce midday sun. Give a liquid feed at half strength every 2 weeks. Spray frequently with a fine mist. Reduce the amount of water gradually as leaf colour fades. Remove dead top growth and overwinter the pots in a dry place.

PROPAGATION Divide the rhizomes in early spring, making sure each section has a growing point, or take 7.5cm/3in stem cuttings in summer, or in early autumn for winter flowering.

SPECIES *Kohleria erianthum (above)*, scarlet flowers spotted red and yellow, dark green leaves clothed with purplish hairs; *K. amabile*, smaller with deep pink flowers spotted purple.

POSSIBLE PROBLEMS Generally trouble-free.

▓ GENERAL TIP

Specializing in one particular family of plants can have absorbing interest and the Gesneraceae (Kohleria and Saintpaulia for example) offer fascinating species for warm locations.

PELARGONIUM

spring to autumn	1.2m/4ft	90cm/3ft	bright	7°C/45°F

Pelargoniums are often called geranium (which is in fact the garden cranesbill). There are a number of species, and many varieties, with an astonishing choice of flower types in shades of white, pink, coral, red and purple.

GENERAL CARE Grow in 10-15cm/4-6in pots of good soil-based compost kept constantly moist while the plants are in active growth. Feed with a high-potash liquid fertilizer every 2 weeks. Place in good light where several hours of direct sunlight (preferably not fierce midday sun) are available every day. Good ventilation is important, especially at high temperatures – pelargoniums positively dislike humidity. Pinch out growing tips to encourage bushy growth. After flowering, cut right back and keep the compost just moist over winter. Repot in spring.

PROPAGATION Sow seed in early spring or take cuttings in the autumn (*see p.14-15*).

VARIETIES Zonal (*above*), potentially very tall, best for conservatories, rounded leaves zoned bronze or wine-red, flowers in umbels: 'Delight', vermilion; 'Maxim Kovaleski', true orange; 'Lady Warwick', white edged red, distinctive blooms; 'Henry Cox', leaves zoned wine-red, red, green and cream. Regal, height up to 60cm/24in, long flowering period, large flowers; 'Black Knight', deep purple edged white; 'Lavender Grand Slam' (*above*); 'Princess of Wales', strawberry pink, frilled petals.

POSSIBLE PROBLEMS Generally trouble-free.

▓ CARE TIP

The winter months can be the most difficult for these plants, and not only because room temperatures are inadequate. More often there is a tendency for the custodian to cut back plants following flowering so that they occupy less storage space in the spare room, or wherever. The result of exposing cut areas late in the year is that rot sets in and ruins the plant.

PRIMULA

| spring | 38cm/15in | 30cm/12in | moderate | 10°C/50°F |

With their primrose-like flowers of yellow, mauve, pink, red, salmon or white, primulas are greatly valued as springtime indoor plants. Plants are usually discarded after flowering, but *Primula obconica* (*above*) can be kept for a second season.

GENERAL CARE Grow in a soil-based compost, using 12.5/5in pots. Stand in moderate light. Room temperature should not exceed 15°C/59°F, preferably less. Keep the compost always moist, not waterlogged, and give a feed of liquid fertilizer every 2 weeks from the time the first flower stalks appear. Pick off faded flowers regularly to ensure a succession of blooms. Repotting is not necessary. To save *P. obconica*, keep cool, just moist and shaded. In the autumn, tidy up the plants and top-dress with fresh compost (*see p.10*).

PROPAGATION Sow fresh seed in early spring. A mid-winter sowing of *P. obconica* will be in full flower a year later and bloom for 6 months in the right conditions.

VARIETIES *P. obconica*, pale green hairy leaves (to which some people are painfully allergic), flowers in clusters; giant-flowered strains are often named for colour, e.g. 'Delicate Pink', 'Red Chief', 'White'; *P. × kewensis*, light green powdered leaves, fragrant yellow flowers; *P. malacoides*, fragrant star-shaped flowers; 'Snowstorm', double white; 'Lilac Queen'.

POSSIBLE PROBLEMS Magnesium deficiency causes yellowing leaves.

■ CARE TIP

Given reasonable care P. obconica will often flower throughout the year. But plants can be a strong irritant to sensitive skin – not only when handling, sometimes being in the same room will induce irritation.

ROSA

| summer | 38cm/15in | 30cm/12in | bright | outdoors |

Miniature roses are descended from *Rosa chinensis* 'Minima', a semi-double China rose still available under the name 'Rouletti'. This variety and others related to it generally reach between 23 and 30cm/9 and 12in. A group of slightly larger miniatures such as 'Starina' (*above*) has been developed, as well as tiny ones like 'Red Elf' (reaches 15cm/6in).

GENERAL CARE Grow in 12.5cm/5in pots of soil-based compost kept nicely moist during the flowering period. At this time, roses need good light and fresh air and are frankly happiest outdoors, being brought in to normal room conditions for short periods. Dead-head regularly and feed with a high-potash fertilizer every 2 weeks. After flowering put the pots outside or in the coldest day-lit spot you have available. Cut all old and damaged stems right back in autumn and top-dress with a 5cm/2in layer of peat to keep the root system from drying out.

PROPAGATION Take cuttings in summer and root in a mixture of equal parts peat and sand. When rooted, pot singly in 7.5cm/3in pots in potting compost.

VARIETIES Tallest: 'Josephine Wheatcroft', semi-double, sunflower yellow; 'Perla de Monserrat', double rose pink; 'Baby Gold Star', semi-double, yellow. Medium: 'Bo-peep', tiny deep pink flowers; 'Granate', velvety deep red, double; Tiny: 'Humpty Dumpty', soft pink; 'Peon', crimson/white eye.

POSSIBLE PROBLEMS Aphids.

■ CARE TIP

Not the easiest of plants for indoors, as they need the lightest possible window in a cool room. As with most flowering plants they need high potash feed which can be found in tomato fertilizer.

RUELLIA

| spring | 90cm/3ft | 60cm/24in | bright | 15°C/59°F |

Ruellias are wonderful plants for winter/spring decoration. With their vivid pink trumpet-shaped flowers and long, pointed green leaves, they have an air of the exotic that enlivens the winter scene. Though tall, they are nicely bushy in shape if the growing tips of young plants are pinched out.

GENERAL CARE Grow in 15cm/6in pots of peat-based compost with the addition of charcoal granules for improved aeraton. Set in a warm room with good light, filtered in high summer. Keep the plants moist at all times, winter included. Repot established specimens in the autumn, but raise new plants annually, as young ones are more productive of flowers. Ruellias that have been repotted should be given a liquid feed at half strength every 2 weeks when in active growth. Immediately after flowering, cut back flowered shoots to within 7.5cm/3in of the surface of the compost.

PROPAGATION When pruning in late spring, take 7.5cm/3in basal cuttings and root them 4 to a 10cm/4in pot of equal parts peat and sand at 21°C/70°F. Pot up singly when growing well.

SPECIES *Ruellia macrantha (above)*, clusters of rose-pink flowers 8cm/3½in long from mid winter to spring; *R. portellae*, small pink flowers from late autumn, beautiful green leaves tinted bronze, veined silver.

POSSIBLE PROBLEMS Plants deteriorate in cold, dry atmospheres.

▨ PROPAGATION TIP

Where space permits it is always wise to have back-up plants of favourite species just in case something goes wrong with the pet plant, or it may be that older ones become ungainly and in need of replacement. Take cuttings of these in spring or early summer, but provide a heated propagator to encourage rooting. One with an electric cable offering bottom heat is ideal.

SAINTPAULIA

| summer | 10cm/4in | 23cm/9in | bright | 13°C/55°F |

African violets, properly called *Saintpaulia ionantha*, belong to the same family as sinningias, achimenes, streptocarpus and kohlerias, all plants noted for their beautiful flowers. They produce blue, purple or pink flowers all year, but mostly in summer. Violet-like, the blooms cluster above a dense rosette of dark green, oval, slightly hairy leaves.

GENERAL CARE Grow in 12.5/5in pots of a peat-based compost kept moist but never waterlogged. Place the pots on saucers of moist pebbles or immersed in larger pots of moist peat. Warmth as well as humidity is essential; the ideal temperature is in the range 18-24°C/64-75°F. Stand in good light, not direct sunlight, and feed with liquid fertilizer at half strength from late spring until flowering stops. Repot at any time, preferably spring, when the plants are pot-bound.

PROPAGATION In summer, take leaf cuttings with a 5cm/2in length of stalk and root in a mixture of equal parts sand and peat at 18-21°C/64-70°F.

VARIETIES 'Diana Blue', velvety royal purple; 'Blue Fairy Tale', rich blue; 'Grandiflora Pink', large-flowered pink.

POSSIBLE PROBLEMS Tarsonemid mites; water on leaves discolours the surface.

▨ FLOWERING TIP

Producing flowers can be a problem – to induce the plant should be in a good light on a windowsill and under a table lamp in the evening. Good light is an important need for flower development.

SINNINGIA

summer	30cm/12in	38cm/15in	bright	15°C/59°F

The showy, trumpet-shaped blooms known commercially as gloxinias are in fact hybrids developed from *Sinningia speciosa*. A wide range is available in a stunning range of colours. The foliage is an added attraction, for the large oval leaves are a fine velvety green.

GENERAL CARE The simplest method of raising gloxinias is to obtain tubers in spring and place them in a bowl of moist peat at 21°C/70°F. Pot them up separately when 5cm/2in high in 15cm/6in pots of peat-based compost; each tuber should be just covered. Grow on in bright light, not direct sunlight, at no less than 18°C/64°F and keep constantly moist. Feed with liquid fertilizer every 2 weeks until flowering is over. Gradually reduce the amount of water as the leaves lose colour. Remove dead top growth, remove tubers from their pots and store over winter in a dry place.

PROPAGATION Divide tubers in spring, making sure each section has at least 2 shoots. Cut them up with a sharp knife, sealing the cut with powdered charcoal. Sinningias may also be raised from seed sown in early spring.

VARIETIES *S. s.* 'Emperor Frederick', scarlet edged white; 'Emperor William', purple edged white; 'Mont Blanc', white.

POSSIBLE PROBLEMS Tubers may rot if overwatered.

▨ GENERAL TIP

When purchasing it is wise to call on the grower of the plant as gloxinia are ill disposed to both packing materials and travelling. Reason for this is the very brittle leaves, and good reason for inspecting the foliage of plants that one intends purchasing to ensure that there are not too many damaged leaves present. Handle with care at all times.

SPATHIPHYLLUM

summer	60cm/24in	60cm/24in	bright	13°C/55°F

Spathiphyllums are related to anthuriums, which they somewhat resemble, but are fortunately rather easier to grow. Known as peace lilies, their white spathes look exquisite against glossy dark green leaves. These blooms may appear at any time in congenial conditions, but most freely in late spring-early summer.

GENERAL CARE Grow in a peat-based loam-free compost kept moist at all times. Warmth and humidity are essential – spray the leaves frequently. Stand the pots in containers of moist peat and position in good light. Feed with liquid fertilizer all year round: every 2 weeks from spring until late summer, monthly at half strength at other times. Reduce the amount of water in winter. Repot every year in spring.

PROPAGATION Divide and replant established specimens in spring.

VARIETIES *Spathiphyllum wallisii* (*above*), only 30cm/12in high, bright green leaves, summer-flowering, will tolerate temperatures down to 10°C/50°F and needs shade in summer; S. × 'Mauna Loa', hybrid of more majestic proportions, large white spathes; needs as much warmth as can be given during spring/summer.

POSSIBLE PROBLEMS Sudden changes in temperature will damage the plant.

▨ CARE TIP

Superb plants with naturally glossy leaves and surprisingly tolerant of room conditions. To maintain appearance the leaves should be periodically cleaned with a soft, moist cloth.

STRELITZIA

| spring | 1.2m/4ft | 90cm/3ft | bright | 10°C/50°F |

The extraordinary shape and colour formation of strelitzia blooms have given this species the popular name bird of paradise. Native to South Africa, *Strelitzia reginae*, *above* (a relative of the banana) bears its flowers in spring: 15cm/6in long, they are orange and blue, rising in a crest from a green bract, and last for several weeks. The mid-green leaves which surround the flowerheads are oval and may be 45cm/18in long. There are no named varieties.

GENERAL CARE Grow in a soil-based compost kept nicely moist throughout the active growing period, and feed with liquid fertilizer every 2 weeks. Situate the plant in bright light where it will receive several hours of direct sunlight every day. The leaves should, however, be protected from very fierce sun. Normal room temperatures are suitable. During the cool of the rest period, let the compost become nearly dry.

PROPAGATION Divide old plants in spring, or detach shoots bearing roots when repotting or just after flowering.

POSSIBLE PROBLEMS Scale insects.

STREPTOCARPUS

| summer | 30cm/12in | 23cm/9in | bright | 10°C/50°F |

In spite of its popular name of Cape primrose, the flowers of *Streptocarpus* × *hybridus* do not resemble primroses at all; they are usually pink, purple, white or blue rather than yellow, and trumpet-shaped. The leaves, however bear some comparison; though those of streptocarpus are relatively large, they are similarly mid-green and corrugated.

GENERAL CARE Streptocarpus do best where they can enjoy high humidity. A well-ventilated greenhouse is the ideal place. Water freely in spring and summer, giving a liquid feed every 2 weeks. A moderately bright position out of direct sunlight will keep plants happy and prevent scorching of the leaves. Remove faded flowerheads. In winter, water sparingly and keep cool. Repot each spring, upgrading by one size until a 20cm/8in pot is reached; simply top-dress with fresh compost annually thereafter (*see p.14*).

PROPAGATION Take leaf cuttings and root in a mixture of equal parts peat and sand at 18°C/64°F or divide established plants in spring or late summer.

VARIETIES *S.* × *h.* 'Constant Nymph', purple-blue flowers; 'Purple Nymph' (*above*), reddish-purple; 'Merton Blue', purplish-blue with white throat.

POSSIBLE PROBLEMS Aphids.

▨ GENERAL TIP

Exotic flowers but unattractive foliage, particularly in older plants. Can be grown from seed but it takes at least four years for flowers to appear, and it may well be ten years!

▨ PROPAGATION TIP

Old-fashioned they may be, but the white and blue varieties of 'Constant Nymph' are still plants worthy of acquiring. If plants are not available acquire a leaf and cut it into sections and stand them upright in peat and sand *mix. Alternatively, cut through the middle of the central vein for its entire length and insert cut edge in same mixture.*

FERNS

If you are sometimes bewildered by the complicated Latin labels given to plants, you should be warned that ferns have the most unpronounceable names. Even a fern-fancier has to be known by the jawbreaking title 'pteropodist'. It sounds prehistoric, but perhaps that is appropriate to families of plants which first appeared hundreds of millions of years ago. They had to wait until the late nineteenth century to be 'discovered' by Victorian plant explorers, who plundered the tropics to fill the ferneries of grand English houses. Some of these fern rooms still exist, havens of green tranquillity; but ferns do not in fact need a special room of their own to thrive – they have not survived the millennia by being over-fussy about their environment.

IDEAL CONDITIONS

Many ferns are hardy in temperate zones and make wonderful garden plants, but those grown as indoor plants are usually of tropical origin. In the wild they grow at the base of trees, terrestrial kinds with their roots in the earth, epiphytic types on the trees themselves with their roots in the rotting vegetation that accumulates in the trees' crevices. They are naturally

The foliage of ferns is seen at its best against a well-lit window.

shielded from the bright light of the sun by foliage above, and enjoy warmth and high humidity. Grown as houseplants they should therefore be protected from scorching sunlight; do not expect them to thrive, however, if permanently placed in deep shade. A certain amount of light is essential for growth. Because the fronds will turn towards the source of light it is a good idea to give the pot a quarter turn every week to prevent uneven development.

The ideal temperature range is between 18 and 21°C/64°F and 70°F (but see individual entries) with humidity correspondingly high and steady. Putting the fern's pot in another, larger one filled with peat kept constantly moist is an excellent solution. Before doing this, however, check that the pot of a newly purchased fern is large enough. Sometimes they need repotting, upgrading by one size. See page 10 for other methods of keeping the humidity level up. Since a great deal of moisture is lost through the delicate fronds, frequent mist-spraying is essential, and the best way to nourish ferns is with a foliar feed, that is, a liquid sprayed on to the foliage.

TRADITIONAL FERNERIES

The Victorians constructed their ferneries as cool, quiet retreats – and bearing in mind some of the gaudier herbaceous borders fashionable at the time, it is easy to see why. The same relaxing atmosphere created by ferns is what endears them to indoor gardeners today. Growing steadily all year (only adiantums positively benefit from a rest), they epitomize calm. Never flowering but always restfully green, ferns look wonderful grouped together, yet each is shapely enough to stand alone. They seem to look equally at home in every room in the house, and to suit cosy room settings as well as more formal designs. Ever-accommodating, ferns make a wonderful background to more colourful plants like tender summer-flowering bulbs, particularly vallotas, or in an arrangement with cyclamens, campanulas and hydrangeas. Those with arching fronds – particularly adiantum, blechnum, davallia, nephrolepis and pellaea – are ideal subjects for hanging baskets.

HANGING BASKET DISPLAYS

Some hanging baskets have a built-in drip tray which stops water getting on to the floor, but you can easily make a drip tray for a traditional wire basket from a large plastic plant saucer. Pierce a number of holes at regular intervals around the rim. Thread wire supports of equal length through the holes and fix them to the basket so that the saucer is about 5cm/2in below it. When filled with water, the dish will provide extra humidity for the plant.

To plant up a wire basket, rest it in a bucket for stability and line with sphagnum moss before filling it with the recommended growing mixture (see individual entries). When holding damp compost and a large plant, the basket will be very heavy and should be attached to fixtures screwed into the ceiling joists.

Hanging baskets are practical as well as decorative, in that they make use of otherwise vacant space and keep plants out of harm's way in busy domestic thoroughfares. The danger is that you will forget to water them, and ferns must be kept constantly moist.

PROPAGATION

Since they never flower, it follows that ferns do not produce seeds. Their method of reproduction is as fascinating as it is complicated, and few amateurs will want to attempt it. Spores, not seeds, contain the germ of a new fern. They are carried in spore cases called sori on the underside of some fronds (visible as dark-coloured dots). When the spores are ripe, the sorus bursts and millions of microscopic spores are scattered. In warmth, moisture and light, a spore will produce an organism called a prothallus, which has both male and female parts. If fertilization occurs, an embryo fern, called a sporophyte, begins to grow. This process takes months, and it is many more before the plantlet achieves a respectable size. Fortunately a number of ferns can be increased relatively easily by dividing the mature plants, and the trusty pteris spreads its spores so freely that you may be given offspring without doing anything at all. For the rest, reproduction from spores is probably best left to the experts.

ADIANTUM

23cm/9in	30cm/12in	moderate	13°C/55°F	high

Adiantums are among the most delicate and decorative ferns. Two types are similar in appearance, with wiry black stems and light green, fan-shaped pinnae; a third species is distinguished by palmate fronds which are reddish-brown when young.

GENERAL CARE Grow in a peat-based compost to which one quarter its volume of sand has been added to improve drainage. Make sure there is a good layer of broken crocks at the bottom of the pot. Keep the compost moist but not water-logged all year round and give a liquid feed every 2 weeks in spring and summer. Withhold fertilizer and reduce the amount of water during the resting period. Adiantum lose their colour if the light is too bright, but should not be placed in full shade. Mist the fronds over daily with tepid boiled water or rainwater if possible. Repot in early spring only if roots can be seen.

PROPAGATION Divide the rhizome into small pieces, each bearing a few fronds, and repot immediately in a compost of equal parts of leaf-mould or peat, loam and coarse sand. Small sections can be broken off when repotting if wished.

VARIETIES *Adiantum capillus veneris* (maidenhair fern, *above*), fragile, fan-shaped pinnae on thin, arching stems; *A. cuneatum* (syn. *A. raddianum*), similar in appearance but slightly larger and coarser; *A. c.* 'Fragrantissima', scented fronds; *A. hispidulum* (rosy maidenhair), fronds reddish when young.

POSSIBLE PROBLEMS Root mealy bugs.

▩ CARE TIP

Perhaps the most popular of all the ferns for indoors – its delicate fronds having great appeal when seen on the retailers' plant benches. Dry air conditions are anathema to their paper-thin foliage, so offer moist surroundings where possible. With age, older fronds lose their appearance and may need to be cut completely away in the autumn to encourage new growth from base.

ASPLENIUM

45cm/18in	60cm/24in	medium	13°C/55°F	high

Asplenium nidus (*above*), popularly known as bird's nest fern, is a native of tropical Asia. Its broad, strap-like fronds of fresh green grow in the form of a rosette, from the centre of which new fronds unfurl. In optimum conditions a frond can reach 1.2m/4ft in length but the dimensions given above are more likely in the home. Even large fronds are relatively fragile, and should be handled as little as possible. There are no named varieties.

GENERAL CARE *Asplenium nidus* is by nature epiphytic (*see p.126*). Grow in a mixture of 2 parts fibrous peat, 1 part loam and 1 part sand. Keep well watered when in active growth and feed with liquid fertilizer at half strength every 2 weeks. Stop feeding during the rest period and keep the compost just moist, but stand the plant in medium light all year round, turning the pot regularly to ensure even growth. Repot, preferably in spring, only when the roots have expanded to fill the pot. Because the roots cling to the side of the pot, it may be necessary to break it to release the root ball.

PROPAGATION This fern can only be raised from spores (*see p.65*).

POSSIBLE PROBLEMS Aphids; scale insects.

▩ CARE TIP

The shuttlecock arrangement of pale green leaves is particularly effective, but leaves should be kept clean by wiping occasionally with a damp cloth. Scale insects (on both sides of leaves) favour aspleniums and should be cleaned off with a firm sponge that has been soaked in insecticide solution. Wear rubber gloves and follow directions for the product.

BLECHNUM

| 38cm/15in | 30cm/12in | bright | 16°C/61°F | moderate |

Blechnums are a large group of arching ferns of different sizes suitable for a number of decorative purposes. The fronds are of the classic fern shape, rather like a nephrolepis.

GENERAL CARE Any good proprietary compost will do, but the best mixture is 2 parts peat (or leaf-mould if available), 1 part loam and 1 part sand, with a good layer of drainage material at the bottom of the pot. The compost should not be packed too tightly around the roots. Do not let the roots dry out at any time. To maintain humidity during the period of active growth, set the pots on saucers of moist pebbles, but do not spray the fronds as this will discolour them. Feed once or twice in summer with liquid fertilizer at half-strength. Give the plants good light, but not direct sunlight. Repot when the roots are visible on the surface of the compost.

PROPAGATION Most species are raised from spores, but sometimes *Blechnum gibbum* produces offsets which can be detached from the parent and potted up. Divide the rhizome of *B. occidentale* and repot each section individually.

SPECIES *B. gibbum*, most common species, shiny green slightly drooping fronds arising from a central rosette; *B. g. tinctum* has young fronds tinged pink. *B. occidentale*, robust species of neat habit.

POSSIBLE PROBLEMS At room temperatures above 21°C/70°F plants suffer serious damage and attack by thrips.

■ CARE TIP

Many ferns suffer indoors because of the dry atmosphere that prevails – to counter such conditions it is wise to plunge the pots in larger pots with damp peat packed around them.

CYRTOMIUM

| 30cm/12in | 45cm/18in | bright | 7°C/45°F | low |

Only one species of cyrtomium is generally available, and one variety in particular is preferred. Known as the holly fern because of the shape of its glossy, leathery pinnae, *Cyrtomium falcatum* 'Rochfordianum' (*above*) is an extremely sturdy rhizomatous plant, which can tolerate low temperatures and humidity. Quick-growing, these handsome plants will continue to thrive even when occasionally subjected to draughts and smoky atmospheres.

GENERAL CARE For all their toughness, holly ferns are not indestructible. They certainly appreciate good light, though not direct sunlight. Grow in a mixture of equal parts of peat, loam and sand, not packed down too tightly in the pot. If steady, normal room temperatures are maintained, no rest period is needed and the compost should be kept nicely moist all year; but if the temperature drops below 13°C/55°F for more than a few days, reduce the amount of water. Give a feed of liquid fertilizer every 2 weeks when in active growth. Repot only when the roots crowd the pot. Plants that have achieved a 15cm/6in pot should simply be top-dressed with fresh compost in early spring (*see p.14*).

PROPAGATION In spring, divide the rhizome into small sections, each bearing healthy roots and a few fronds. Pot up in 7.5cm/3in pots of the recommended mixture kept barely moist until well rooted. Thereafter treat as mature plants.

POSSIBLE PROBLEMS Generally trouble-free.

■ DESIGN TIP

The Holly Fern is very distinctive among this type of plant, having foliage with a naturally high gloss. The latter is ever an advantage with plants that are used for indoor decoration. When arranged in groups with other house plants that have more colourful variegated foliage the contrast improves the appearance of all the plants in the arrangement.

DAVALLIA

| 45cm/18in | 45cm/18in | bright | 5°C/41°F | moderate |

There are three species of davallia in common use, fine ferns with densely clustered, delicate triangular fronds of pale or medium green. All grow from rhizomes.

GENERAL CARE Grow in a mixture of 3 parts peat, 1 part leaf-mould and 1 part sand, with plenty of drainage material at the bottom of the pot. Keep the compost consistently moist, not waterlogged, during the period of active growth and feed with liquid fertilizer every 2 weeks. Do not spray the foliage. Keep the compost just moist during the winter. Place the plants where they will receive bright light, but not direct sunlight. They are happiest at normal room temperatures but will tolerate cooler conditions and low humidity. Repot small davallias in spring, trimming the roots and detaching a few sections of rhizome.

PROPAGATION Cut off tip sections of rhizome to which 2 fronds are attached. Place in 7.5cm/3in pots containing a mixture of equal parts peat and sand, pinning them to the surface with wire. Enclose in plastic bags until rooted. Gradually acclimatize to normal conditions and pot up after 3 months.

SPECIES *D. canariensis* (hare's foot fern, *above*), creeping scaly rhizomes covered with soft grey fur explain the common name, medium green fronds; *D. fijiensis*, very light green elegant fronds; *D. f. plumosa* is a feathery type; *D. mariesii*, pretty, dwarf, fully hardy species 15cm//6in high, light green fronds.

POSSIBLE PROBLEMS Generally trouble-free.

▓ PROPAGATION TIP

The custom of placing propagating material in polythene bags when propagating is to reduce transpiration and so stop the potting material from drying out. It is suitable for most plants.

NEPHROLEPIS

| 60cm/24in | 90cm/3ft | moderate | 10°C/50°F | moderate |

Of all the ferns used for indoor decoration, the nephrolepis in its various forms is the most important, and one of the most beautiful when in good health. Popularly known as the ladder fern, *Nephrolepis exaltata* (*above*) produces graceful, arching fronds of bright green, best appreciated when the plant is placed on a pedestal, or, if it is not too large, in a hanging basket.

GENERAL CARE Grow in a mixture of 3 parts fibrous peat, 2 parts loam and 1 part sand and keep well watered. Give a liquid feed every 4 weeks. Nephrolepis like normal room temperatures, but above 21°C/70°F the fronds will appreciate mist-spraying with tepid boiled water or rainwater. These plants are in active growth all year and like a position enjoying good light, though not direct sunlight. Repot in spring when the roots have filled the pot, upgrading by one size. When plants have reached the largest convenient pot size, trim the roots lightly and replace in the cleaned pot with fresh compost.

PROPAGATION Plantlets are formed from runners. Detach the young plants and pot up in peat and sand at 13°C/55°F until rooted.

VARIETIES *N. a.* 'Bostoniensis' (Boston fern), quick-growing, with broad fronds; 'Whitmanii', feathery fronds; 'Hillii', crinkled, pale fronds.

POSSIBLE PROBLEMS In high temperatures where the atmosphere is dry, fronds will turn yellow and shrivel up.

▓ PROPAGATION TIP

To propagate plants from the naturally developing runners the growing pot should be plunged in a roomy box of peat so that runners can be pegged down in the peat to root and establish.

PELLAEA

| 45cm/18in | 60cm/24in | bright | 7°C/45°F | moderate |

There are many species of pellaea, small- to medium-sized ferns best suited to hanging baskets. The stalks are wiry, rising from rhizomes set just below the surface of the mixture.

GENERAL CARE Grow in a light, porous mixture composed of 2 parts peat, 1 part loam and 1 part sand. Do not let the roots dry out at any time: since pellaeas do not need a rest period, water moderately all year and give a liquid feed every 4 weeks. Do not spray the fronds. Give the plants a position in good light, out of direct sunlight. Repot in spring when the roots fill the pot.

PROPAGATION When the plants have reached pots of 20cm/8in, divide the rhizome into small sections, each bearing healthy roots and a few fronds, and pot up in the recommended mixture.

SPECIES *Pellaea rotundifolia* (button fern, *above*), almost round, tiny pinnae on long arching fronds. Good for ground cover in mixed plantings as it likes the humidity created by other plants; fronds trail over the side of the pot. Shallow-rooting, grow in half-pots. *P. viridis* (green cliffbrake), sometimes listed as a species of pteris, a bushy plant with upright, vivid green triangular fronds each up to 75cm/30in long and deeply divided.

POSSIBLE PROBLEMS Generally trouble-free.

PHYLLITIS

| 60cm/24in | 20cm/8in | medium | 7°C/45°F | moderate |

One species of phyllitis, *Phyllitis scolopendrium* (the hart's tongue fern), is in general cultivation. A hardy, rhizomatous plant which can be grown in the garden, it will tolerate cool rooms as long as there is sufficient light. The strap-like, bright green fronds unfurl from a central rosette. A number of different blade forms are displayed in the varieties.

GENERAL CARE Grow in a mixture of 2 parts leaf-mould or peat, 1 part loam and 1 part sand. Keep the mixture just moist, reducing the amount of water if the temperature drops below 13°C/55°F for more than a few days. Give a liquid feed at half-strength every 2 weeks all year round. Repot only when the roots fill the pot, placing the rhizomes vertically. When the largest suitable pot size has been reached, trim away up to one-third of the rootball and replace in the cleaned pot with fresh mixture.

PROPAGATION In spring, cut off small sections of rhizome bearing a few fronds and insert in 7.5cm/3in pots of the standard mixture. Keep just moist until new fronds develop, then treat as mature plants. Sometimes bulbils form on the fronds or at the base of the fronds; these can be detached and grown on.

VARIETIES *P. s.* 'Crispum', blades bright green with wavy or ruffled edges; *P. s.* 'Cristatum', frilly blades with crested tips.

POSSIBLE PROBLEMS Generally trouble-free.

■ CARE TIP

Many of the ferns are sensitive to the use of chemicals on their foliage, and to overdoses of fertilizer when feeding. One way of overcoming these difficulties is to use a slow release fertilizer in tablet form pressed into the pot soil for feeding and to employ impregnated fertilizer pins pressed into the soil to control many of the pests. Both treatments are clean and effective.

■ PLANTING TIP

Tougher ferns such as the scolopendrium will benefit from a holiday in the garden during the summer. Choose a lightly shaded location and plunge plant pots in moist peat.

PLATYCERIUM

60cm/24in	60cm/24in	bright	13°C/55°F	moderate

Platycerium bifurcatum (*above*) is an epiphytic fern (*see p.64*) which in its native Australia grows in the upper branches of trees, clinging to the bark by means of a single, sterile frond. From this, fertile fronds of mid-green overlaid with silver hairs arise, which divide at the end to look like antlers – hence the common name, stag's horn fern.

GENERAL CARE The best way to display these extraordinary plants is to wire them to a piece of bark wrapped in sphagnum moss and hang them up where they will receive bright light (not direct sunlight) in an airy room. A temperature of about 21°C/70°F is best in summer; higher than that, humidity must be correspondingly increased. To water, submerge the bark and sterile frond in a bucket of water for 15 minutes once a week, allowing it to drain before rehanging. Follow the same procedure during the rest period, but only leave the plant in water for 2-3 minutes. Do not wipe the fronds – in fact, try not to touch them at all. To clean them, spray very occasionally with a fine mist of cooled boiled water or rainwater.

PROPAGATION Detach young plants from the stems and attach them to fresh pieces of bark.

VARIETIES *P. b.* 'Majus', leathery fronds with fewer incisions than the species.

POSSIBLE PROBLEMS Generally trouble-free.

▓ DESIGN TIP

Majestic plants when grown with care. Oddly, the anchor fronds that form at the base and secure it naturally to its anchorage will grow apace on natural materials, but not so on plastic pots!

POLYPODIUM

90cm/3ft	60cm/24in	medium	7°C/45°F	moderate

There are numerous species of polypodium cultivated in gardens, though only one, *Polypodium aureum* (syn. *Phlebodium aureum*, *above*) is used for indoor decoration. It is commonly called hare's foot fern (like davallia, which has very different fronds), because of the creeping rhizomes with furry scales.

GENERAL CARE Grow in a mixture of equal parts of peat, loam and sand in a wide, shallow pot to accommodate the rhizomatous network. Water well, and give a liquid feed at half-strength every 2 weeks. Keep the plants out of direct sunlight, which will scorch the leaves, but in good light all year round. Normal room temperatures are best; if the temperature exceeds 21°C/70°F for several days increase the humidity by placing the pots in saucers of moist pebbles, and spray the fronds lightly with a very fine mist. Repot in spring.

PROPAGATION Cut off 7.5cm/3in sections from the tips of the rhizome and place on the surface of the standard mixture in small pots. Peg down each section, moisten the compost and place the pots in plastic bags in the warmth until rooting has taken place. Gradually acclimatize to normal conditions and then treat as mature plants.

VARIETIES *P. a. areolatum*, leathery, blue-green fronds; *P. a. mayi*, wavy fronds of silvery green, veins tinted purple.

POSSIBLE PROBLEMS Generally trouble-free.

▓ DESIGN TIP

The greenhouse fernery is a very tranquil and soothing sort of environment – to emulate in some small degree indoors it is worth offering ferns a corner of their own in which to grow.

POLYSTICHUM

90cm/3ft	60cm/24in	moderate	7°C/45°F	moderate

There are a number of polystichums cultivated in gardens. The best for indoor use is *Polystichum setiferum* (*above*), the soft shield fern, which is an adaptable species tolerant of low temperatures. It is a handsome plant with abundant foliage and looks splendid alone or in a collection of ferns. The fronds are long, strap-like and deeply divided, soft in texture and not glossy.

GENERAL CARE Grow in a mixture of equal parts of leaf-mould or peat, loam and coarse sand, never allowing the mixture to dry out. At temperatures above 18°C/65°F, increase humidity by standing the pots in saucers of moist pebbles ad spraying the fronds with a very fine spray of cooled boiled water or rainwater. Feed with liquid fertilizer at half-strength every 4 weeks. Plants grow all year, and need good light (not direct sunlight) at all times; normal room temperatures are suitable. Repot in spring if the roots fill the pot.

PROPAGATION In spring, divide the rhizomes into smaller sections with a sharp knife and repot in the recommended mixture, setting each piece horizontally and only half-covered by the compost.

VARIETIES *P. s.* 'Plumoso-divisilobum', very finely divided, exquisitely delicate fronds up to 60cm/24in long, spreading up to 1.2m/4ft.

POSSIBLE PROBLEMS Generally trouble-free.

▦ CARE TIP

Ferns are seldom seen at their best when growing in tiny pots that restrict their development, however, continual potting-on means that they require ever more space in which to be housed. Where space is available plants can be potted on into a quite large container, but this is usually a two-handed task to reduce the likelihood of plants being damaged.

PTERIS

45cm/18in	38cm/15in	bright	7°C/45°F	high

Pteris species are collectively known as table ferns. All produce numerous clumps of fronds from rhizomes.

GENERAL CARE Grow in a mixture of equal parts of peat, loam and sand and keep well watered at all times. Pteris are in active growth all year, and like normal room temperatures. Give the fronds a misting over with tepid boiled water or rainwater if the temperature rises above 18°C/65°F for more than 2 days. Feed with half-strength liquid fertilizer every 4 weeks. Set the pots in good light (not direct sunlight) and give them a quarter-turn every day to ensure even growth. Repot when the roots fill the pot: in spring, transfer the plants to a pot one size larger, just burying the rhizome.

PROPAGATION In spring, cut the rhizome into 7.5cm/3in sections, each bearing both roots and a clump of fronds. Plant up in the recommended mixture and treat as mature plants. Pteris spread their spores freely, and you may well find tiny ferns which may be potted up in 5cm/2in pots and grown on.

VARIETIES *Pteris cretica* (ribbon fern), light to medium green fronds with wiry black stalks and strap-shaped pinnae which in the variety 'Albolineata' (*above*) are marked with a creamy central band; the fronds of 'Wilsonii' are crested at the tip. *P. ensiformis*, species with finer, deep green fronds.

POSSIBLE PROBLEMS Outer fronds of mature plants dry up. Cut them away at the base.

▦ CARE TIP

These are almost invariably purchased when growing in relatively small pots – often with a great deal of top growth. Such plants should have their roots examined on getting them home with a view to potting on the plant if, as is probable, there is a mass of congested brown roots in evidence. The new pot should offer at least 2cm (1in) of free space all the way round.

PALMS

Palms are the aristocrats of indoor plants. They have the dignified air of trees, and in their natural habitat, the tropics, most would of course grow into tall trees in time. Those available in plant centres are relatively young, but even so are the result of years of careful work by the nurseryman. Because it takes so much time and care to raise palms from seed, they are very expensive to buy, and only a small proportion of the large number growing in the wild are accorded this treatment. Despite their special status, however, palms are not fussy as houseplants. With attention to a few simple points, they will thrive for years, becoming a permanent feature of an interior design just as trees do in the outdoor garden.

KEEPING PALMS INDOORS

Many palms look different in their juvenile form from the way they do in maturity. Unlike an apple tree, which even at a year old is recognizably the precursor of a mature productive specimen, young palms are not miniature versions of their older selves. Most obviously, they do not have a long trunk, though some have a short stem; the leaves are naturally smaller, no flowers bloom (with the exception of chamaedorea, which may flower at about six years old) and therefore no fruit is produced. You will not be gathering your own dates and coconuts!

Unless kept in a special house in a botanical garden, palms are unlikely to achieve maturity for the many years of their life indoors, and this is to your advantage – no conventional room could accommodate them if they did. In the juvenile state, palms would naturally be protected from the sun's intense heat by the leaves of mature trees. It makes sense to imitate these conditions at home, placing palms in bright light that is filtered by a fine curtain. They can withstand a few hours of direct sunlight, however; and those which are usually

The sumptuous and exotic furnishings of this Eastern-inspired room need rather special plants. Palms have just the right combination of grace and flamboyance to work well with all the mirror, gilt and silk surfaces, without being too fussy.

positioned in poor light will certainly benefit from being moved outside on warm days – if they are not too heavy to lift. While palms can tolerate a degree of dryness in the air, the fronds look fresher in a slightly humid atmosphere and the possibility of infestation by red spider mite is reduced. The best way to achieve humidity is to stand the pots on trays of moist pebbles while the palms are in active growth. You can test humidity with a hygrometer.

TIPS FOR GOOD HEALTH

As important design features, if not for the sake of their health, palms should be kept clean. Sponge each frond by hand with tepid water, or place the whole plant in the bath and shower the leaves or move it outside if there is a warm summer shower of rain. Requirements for water vary (see individual entries) but generally the compost should be kept moist throughout the growing period. Always check the compost before watering, however; overwatering is the greatest single cause of damage to palms.

A winter rest period is essential; during this time palms can tolerate temperatures down to 13°C/55°F or 7°C/45°F depending on species, require very little water and no feeding. Do not automatically repot your palms in spring; the longer you can keep them in their present pot the better, to keep size within reasonable bounds. Repot – in spring – only when the pot is completely filled with roots.

Repotting is the time to detach suckers, if any, and take advantage of a natural method of propagation, since raising palms from seed cannot be achieved by the amateur. Suckers are produced by chamaerops, chrysalidocarpus and phoenix. After separating the sucker from its parent, pot it up in a moistened mixture of equal parts of peat and sand. Enclose the pot in a plastic bag secured with a rubber band. Stand in bright filtered light and keep warm – not less than 21°C/70°F. Rooting may take up to twelve weeks. Do not let the compost dry out during this time, and shake off any condensation that forms inside the bag. New top growth indicates that rooting has occurred. At this point, remove the bag, keep the plant lightly watered and feed with liquid fertilizer every four weeks. The following spring, pot up in the recommended growing mixture.

SITING PALMS

Even in youth, palms are impressive plants and some eventually reach the ceiling. This is the most important factor to be taken into account when deciding where to site them. In a small room with pale walls, good light and simple furniture, a single palm makes a striking feature. Only much larger rooms can accommodate a group of palms, for example a spacious porch, drawing room or conservatory. Keep the containers ultra-simple. As palms should not be situated where they are likely to be damaged, a busy kitchen or family sitting room is probably not a good choice. The beautiful shape of palm fronds is undoubtedly best appreciated against a pale, plain background. Having said that, they share with ferns the ability to combine gracefully with other plants. A stately palm could be the centre-piece of a group which included achimenes, cyclamen or sinningia, bushy in shape with foliage beautiful enough to hold its own. If you are lucky enough to have the space for it, such an arrangement would be the epitome of an indoor garden.

Palms add style and elegance to any interior. The most commonly grown indoor form is Howeia forsteriana. *When it reaches about this size, it makes a perfect floor-standing specimen. The wicker-basket container works well in this situation but any large, simple container would look good. In a period setting an elaborate cachepot would be particularly effective.*

CHAMAEDOREA

| 60cm/24in | 38cm/15in | medium | 13°C/55°F | moderate |

The parlour palm, *Chamaedorea elegans* (syn. *Neanthe bella*, *above*), is one of the easiest palms to grow and much smaller than most others. The upright fronds are light and feathery. Young plants may produce small yellow-green flowers, which should be removed. No named varieties are available.

GENERAL CARE Grow in a mixture of 2 parts peat, 1 part loam and 1 part sand, and keep the compost thoroughly moist, not waterlogged, at all times. Chamaedoreas continue to grow all year, though more slowly in winter, when watering should be reduced slightly. Give a liquid feed at half-strength every 4 weeks. Temperatures in the range 18-24°C/65-75°F are best, with humidity provided by regularly spraying the leaves. Stand the pots in saucers of damp pebbles. Sponge the leaves with tepid water to clean them. In their natural habitat these small palms are shielded from the sun by taller trees: as house plants they need good light but not direct sunlight. Repot carefully when the roots fill the pot, upgrading by one size and adding peat or leaf-mould to the mixture.

PROPAGATION Chamaedoreas are best raised from seed, but this is a very lengthy process.

POSSIBLE PROBLEMS Red spider mite.

CHAMAEROPS

| 1,2m/4ft | 90cm/3ft | bright | 10°C/50°F | moderate |

Chamaerops humilis, the European fan palm, *above*, is the only palm native to Europe. It is found in Mediterranean countries, varying greatly in size according to conditions. In the home it needs bright light, including 3-4 hours of direct sunlight every day. It needs space, too, in which to spread its arching fronds, and makes a statuesque contribution to a room setting.

GENERAL CARE Grow in a soil-based compost to which a little leaf-mould, if available, has been added. Keep well-watered, but do not let the pot stand in water. Feed with liquid fertilizer every 2 weeks when in active growth. Normal room temperatures are suitable. During the cooler rest period, water very sparingly. Repot every other spring until the palm is in a 30cm/12in pot. Simply top-dress with fresh compost in subsequent years (*see p.10*).

PROPAGATION Detach basal suckers from the stem whenever they appear, making sure healthy roots are attached to each. Set in small pots of the recommended compost kept just moist, warm and in good light until new growth appears. Thereafter treat as mature plants.

VARIETIES *C. h. argentea*; silvery green foliage; *C. h. elegans*; a slender, graceful form.

POSSIBLE PROBLEMS Red spider mite; leaf tips turn brown with sudden variations in temperature.

▦ GENERAL TIP

The parlour palm is the best selection for smaller rooms. When purchasing, it is wise to seek plants that have numerous growing stems in the pot as opposed to single ones.

▦ GENERAL TIP

Hardy in sheltered areas, the European Palm is only suitable where there is ample space. In its favour, however, it is very tough and able to tolerate low room or conservatory temperatures.

CHRYSALIDOCARPUS

1.8m/6ft	90cm/3ft	bright	15°C/59°F	moderate

Variously known as the butterfly palm or areca palm, *Chrysalidocarpus lutescens* (*above*) is a native of India with slender, upright fronds. The description suffix *lutescens* means yellow, referring to the golden tinge of both stalks and foliage. This beautiful but rather slow-growing palm produces numerous small suckers at the base. There is only one species, and no named varieties.

GENERAL CARE Grow in a soil-based compost kept constantly moist. Feed with liquid fertilizer every two weeks. Normal room temperatures are suitable, and the plant should be positioned where it receives direct sunlight, filtered through a fine curtain. Clean the leaves with a spray mist or by standing the plant outside in a gentle summer shower. Repot every other year until the largest convenient pot size has been achieved, and simply topdress annually thereafter.

PROPAGATION In spring, detach basal suckers when 30cm/12in high and bearing some roots. Plant up individually in a 2:1 mixture of compost and sand, transferring to pots of the standard mixture after 1 year.

POSSIBLE PROBLEMS Scale insects; red spider mite.

COCOS

1.8m/6ft	1.2m/4ft	bright	16°C/61°F	high

The small, decorative plant known as the coconut palm is usually available at about 30cm/12in high, and it takes many years to reach the mature height given above. Its small size makes it useful as a house plant, but it needs particular conditions to do well.

GENERAL CARE Grow in a soil-based compost and water liberally from spring to autumn, gradually reducing the amount of water over a period of four weeks until during the winter rest period the compost is kept barely moist. When in active growth give a liquid feed at half-strength every three weeks. At this time the ideal temperature is 21°C/70°F; bright light and high humidity are essential. Spray the fronds frequently and stand the pots in saucers of moist pebbles. Repot as growth begins in spring; this should not be necessary more often than every three years.

PROPAGATION Coconut palms are raised from seed in high temperatures and in high humidity, conditions which the amateur is unlikely to be able to provide.

SPECIES There is only one species correctly known as *Syagrus weddeliana*, but always sold as *Cocos weddeliana* (*above*). The true coconut palm grown commercially for its fruit is *C. nucifera*.

POSSIBLE PROBLEMS Generally trouble-free.

▓ SPECIAL CARE TIP

Do not be deceived by the yellow leaves of this plant which could mistakenly give the impression that the specimen is suffering from an iron deficiency. Do not treat as for this.

▓ GENERAL TIP

Grown indoors, the coconut palm does not produce fruit and is in fact very short lived, lasting only one or two years. You can try propagating from a fresh coconut – it will sprout roots and leaves from the same eye – by putting the fruit in damp sphagnum moss at a temperature of 20-25°C (68°-77°F).

CYCAS

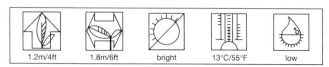

1.2m/4ft	1.8m/6ft	bright	13°C/55°F	low

Cycas revoluta is generally known as the sago palm. Cycas is the Greek word for palm, but in spite of its name and its palm-like appearance this plant is in fact a cycad, a very primitive plant type. Slow-growing, it produces arching fronds of many fine segments arising from a central base which looks rather like a pineapple. The graceful outline of the cycas belies its tough nature. As long as light is good, it is very tolerant of otherwise poor conditions. There are no named varieties.

GENERAL CARE Grow in a mixture of two parts soil-based compost to 1 part coarse sand, with the rounded base – actually a swollen stem – sitting on the surface. The base acts as a reservoir for water. Cycases are in active growth virtually all year, and need constant good light. Water moderately and give a liquid feed every four weeks; if poor winter light results in a period of rest, water sparingly and cease feeding. Slow growth means that repotting should not be necessary more often than every three years.

PROPAGATION Cycases are raised from seed, a lengthy process not recommended for amateurs.

POSSIBLE PROBLEMS Overwatering causes brown spots on the leaves; underwatering turns them yellow. Any disfigured leaves should be removed immediately.

■ SPECIAL CARE TIP

New leaves arrive curled like new fern leaves and gradually both the stem and new leaves uncurl from the base to the tip. Take extra care as these leaves are very delicate and easily damaged.

HOWEA

3m/10ft	1.2m/4ft	medium	10°C/50°F	moderate

Howeas are slow-growing palms that eventually reach stately proportions, but even when young they have a dignified and formal beauty. The two species commonly available are tall with slender stems from which dark green, deeply cut fronds arise.

GENERAL CARE Grow in a soil-based compost and give moderate amounts of cooled boiled water or rainwater during the period of active growth, with a liquid feed every 2 weeks. To clean the leaves, sponge or spray them with water, or stand them outside in a summer shower. Do not use any of the proprietary leaf polishes. They thrive at a sunless window or in bright light; in direct sunlight or deep shade they will deteriorate. Normal room temperatures are suitable and low levels of humidity are tolerated. Repot every other spring, up-grading by one size, and firming the compost well around the roots. Provide a good layer of drainage material at the bottom of the pot.

PROPAGATION Howeas are raised from seed, a lengthy and demanding process.

SPECIES *Howea belmoreana*, the typical palm-court palm, imposing but graceful even when it reaches full size; *H. forsteriana*, a lower-growing species more suitable for the home, but because the leaflets are held horizontally the spread is considerable and it still needs plenty of space.

POSSIBLE PROBLEMS Red spider mite; tap water, or too much water of any kind, results in brown spots on the leaves.

■ CARE TIP

The tall and stately kentia palm is often sold in pots of soil in which there is little root development. This can be an advantage as it obviates the need for potting on the plant for two, possibly three years. But there is a disadvantage with weakly rooted plants in that they are easily detached from the soil if lifted by the stems – lift by grasping the pot.

PHOENIX

1.8m/6ft | 90cm/3ft | bright | 7°C/45°F | low

The three date palms favoured for indoor decoration are handsome species with arching pinnate fronds. They are slow-growing, and will take some years to reach their maximum size.

GENERAL CARE Grow in a soil-based compost kept constantly moist during the period of active growth. Feed with liquid fertilizer every 2 weeks. Phoenix species are happy in normally warm room temperatures in full light. When temperatures begin to fall and the plants enter the dormant period, gradually reduce the amount of water until the compost is kept just moist. Repot every 2 or 3 years, progressing to a pot 5cm/2in larger each time. When repotting, firm the compost down well and leave a good margin between the surface and the pot rim.

PROPAGATION Date palms are usually grown from seed, which is a very long process. It is sometimes possible to remove rooted suckers from *Phoenix roebelenii* and grow them on in 7.5cm/3in pots of the standard mixture.

SPECIES *P. canariensis* (Canary date palm), a robust and popular species, with stiff green pinnae arranged herringbone fashion on arching stems; *P. roebelinii* (pigmy date palm, *above*), max height 90cm/3ft with delicate, arching fronds. This species requires filtered light. *P. dactylifera* (true date palm), blue-green, prickly fronds; faster-growing and generally less fine than the other two.

POSSIBLE PROBLEMS Scale insects; mealy bugs.

■ CARE TIP

These develop into bold plants with rough stems that make it essential that they should be potted into heavier clay pots as they increase in size. The clay pot will give the plant much better anchorage while indoors, but more so if it is to spend some of the summer months on the patio outside. Larger plants require careful handling.

TRACHYCARPUS

2.4m/8ft | 2m/6ft | bright | 7°C/45°F | moderate

A native of China, *Trachycarpus fortunei (above)* is commonly known either as the chusan palm, or the windmill palm, from the shape of its fan-like fronds, which when fully developed are separated into distinct, narrow segments. In temperate zones it may be grown outside, where it may exceed the height given above. In the home, however, confined to a pot, growth is slow and plant size manageable. An average height of 1.2m/4ft is likely. There is a dwarf species, *T. f. surculosus*, which seldom exceeds 60cm/24in.

GENERAL CARE Grow in soil-based compost, kept constantly moist during the period of active growth. Chusan palm is one of the hardier kinds which can tolerate low winter temperatures, preferring normal room temperatures when actively growing. During this period give a liquid feed every four weeks. Good light is important, and some direct sunlight every day will be appreciated. As the leaves mature the colour fades to brown, and they can be pulled away or cut off. Repot when the roots have filled the pot – about every three years – placing a 5cm/2in layer of drainage material in the bottom of the new pot.

PROPAGATION *T. fortunei* is raised from seed, which is a lengthy affair. *T. f. surculosus* produces suckers which can be detached in spring and potted up.

POSSIBLE PROBLEMS Red spider mite.

■ ORGANIC TIP

The Trachycarpus has a useful advantage over other palms in that it will happily occupy a place on the patio during all but the coldest months making an attractive addition to the garden.

BULBS

At the mention of flowering bulbs, inevitably one thinks of spring, with daffodils and crocuses in bloom. But there are bulbs which bloom in all seasons; not only that, growing bulbs indoors means that tender species can be raised which will flower over several years. Species which are hardy enough to flower outside such as narcissi and iris usually spend only one flowering season indoors; these may be thought of as temporary indoor plants. Permanent, tender species include the fabulous crinum and vallota, both from South Africa, and ever-popular hippeastrums, from South America. Despite their exotic origins, none requires excessively high temperatures and are easy to grow indoors.

A bulb is constructed as a series of tightly overlapping leaves – as can be seen by slicing vertically into an onion – forming a storage organ for food and water and sending out fine roots from the base. Corms are modified stems which act in the same way. Buy fresh bulbs from a reputable supplier and plant them at the recommended time for the best results. They will have been raised at the correct pace and temperature to produce beautiful blooms.

GROWING HARDY BULBS INDOORS

Crocuses, narcissi, tulips, hyacinths and iris, which are all familiar spring-flowering garden bulbs, can be induced to flower in winter to provide indoor decorations. Specially prepared bulbs are recommended for this treatment. They will only flower once indoors, but will do so again if planted outside. Sometimes they skip a season while building up food supplies, then go on to bloom for several years. If you do not have a garden, pass the bulbs on to someone who does.

Bulbs for forcing are usually available in late summer/early autumn. Buy from a shop where they have been kept cool. Choose firm, clean specimens with no sign of root or shoot development. Potting compost is necessary if you plan to set the bulbs outdoors afterwards. If not, bulb fibre – which contains no nutrients – may be used, and the bowl need not have any drainage holes.

If you wish to keep bulbs for outdoor planting, remove faded flowerheads only, allowing the leaves and stems to die down naturally. Keep the bowls in a light place at about 4–7°C/39–45°F and water them regularly. In spring, remove the bulbs and their compost from the bowl and plant out the clump 15cm/6in deep.

Hyacinths and tazetta narcissi can be grown in water only in specially designed glass vases. This is an unusually attractive way of displaying bulbs which holds great charm for children. The bulb should fit snugly into the bowl of the vase with its base just touching the water – no deeper, or it will rot. Top up as necessary. Use specially prepared bulbs and start them off at any time from late summer to late autumn. Keep in a cool place – dark for hyacinths, well-lit for narcissi – until the roots are about 7.5cm/3in long and the leaves peeping through the neck of the bulb. Thereafter treat as bulbs grown in compost, with the difference that, having been deprived of food, these bulbs will not be any good for planting outdoors.

Because flowers last longer in cool rooms, forced bulbs are ideal to brighten a well-lit hall or landing, or set in the light of a shady, cool window. While you can plant bulbs singly, they invariably look best in groups, larger species such as hyacinths, some tulips and narcissi in sets of three or five. Increase the numbers for smaller narcissi such as 'Silver Chimes' and miniatures such as crocus and *Iris reticulata*. All can be planted close together, and this gives a more luxuriant effect when in bloom. If you have the space, it is well worth planting in succession so that you will have flowers in the house over many weeks.

The hippeastrum hybrids, popularly known as amaryllis, are striking by any standards and constantly gaining in popularity.

GROWING TENDER BULBS

The three tender bulbs described in this chapter are all members of the amaryllis family, with strap-like leaves and fabulous lily-like blooms borne on long straight stems. Hippeastrums are the first to bloom, the numerous hybrids in very early spring. The colour choice includes all shades of pink and red as well as white. Because specially prepared bulbs can be forced rather as hardy bulbs are, but without a necessary cold, dark period, you can pot up several at staggered intervals to ensure a succession of blooms. As well as the hybrids, try to obtain bulbs of the true species such as *H. aulicum*, which bears huge red flowers in winter or the exquisite *H. candidum*, which may reach 90cm/3ft and bears huge, drooping, scented white flowers tinted green – a stunning plant for a conservatory or sunny porch. It flowers in summer. *H. reticulatum*, about 45cm/18in high, will continue the display into the autumn, if given warmth, with pink flowers and leaves striped white. Crinums, at 1.2m/4ft high when fully mature, are another good choice for a conservatory. Large, eye-catching plants need a spacious setting not only to look their best but to prevent damage to the petals and stems. Like vallotas, crinums bloom in summer, providing a colourful and exotic display for many weeks.

Tender bulbs flower year after year if properly treated, and then obligingly produce offsets to ensure a supply after the parent is exhausted. After flowering time, the aim is to build up a fresh store of nourishment in the bulb. Remove each flower as it fades, but let the foliage die down naturally – do not be tempted to tie it into a bunch for the sake of neatness – and cut off the flower stem cleanly when it is yellow and limp. Plants should be fed regularly during active growth and until all flowers have faded; then stop, and gradually reduce the amount of water until the compost is just moist (let it dry for hippeastrums). After the recuperative dormant period, the cycle begins again.

PROPAGATION

Detach offsets at repotting time. Knock the plant and all the compost clinging to the bulbs out of the pot. Ease off the compost and separate the offsets from the parent carefully, without damaging the roots. Pot up singly in suitably sized pots and grow on as mature plants. They will not reach full size for a year or two. Even so, raising plants in this way is very rewarding and an unmissable opportunity to increase your stock at minimal cost.

CRINUM

summer/autumn	1.2m/4ft	bright	10°C/50°F	low

Crinums or swamp lilies are natives of South Africa, and bear clusters of stunning lily-like flowers of pink, white or red at the top of strong straight stems, surrounded by strap-like leaves. Large, eye-catching plants, they need a spacious setting to be fully appreciated.

GENERAL CARE Plant large bulbs in a soil-based compost in pots no more than 5cm/2in greater in diameter than the bulbs themselves. Smaller bulbs may be set 3 to a 20cm/8in pot. Water well during active growth, but do not let the pots stand in water. Give a liquid feed every 3 weeks. Stand the plants where they will receive 2-3 hours of direct sunlight every day. Normal room temperatures are suitable. The plants rest at lower temperatures in mid winter. As the leaves become tired they fall or may be picked off, and new ones will appear. Repot as infrequently as possible; crinums do best when they are undisturbed. When necessary, repot in spring.

PROPAGATION Remove offsets when repotting over-crowded clumps and pot up firmly (individually or 3 to a suitable-sized pot). Water sparingly for 4-6 weeks then treat as mature bulbs.

SPECIES *Crinum × powellii* (*above*), hybrid form, trumpet-shaped flowers of deep pink, green at the base; abundant foliage. *C. bulbispermum*, slender, narrow leaves, huge white flowers flushed pink.

POSSIBLE PROBLEMS Bulb mites.

▧ CARE TIP

Depending on variety these may be tender bulbs for the heated greenhouse or, in the case of C. powellii, they may be hardy and planted at the base of a sunny wall. During their rest period, bulbs should be stored in a heated greenhouse by laying their pots on their sides under the greenhouse staging – in this position water is prevented from getting into pots.

CROCUS

spring	7.5cm/3in	bright	13°C/55°F	low

There are a number of garden crocuses which bloom at different times of year, but the best forms for indoor cultivation are spring-flowering Dutch hybrids. These corms bear very large flowers which may be white, yellow or purple. Do not mix different colours in the same container as they come into flower at different times; a splash of a single colour lasting a few weeks is much more effective.

GENERAL CARE Plant the corms in a container of soil-based compost in the autumn, water very lightly and keep cool and dark, preferably burying them outside. Bring inside in late winter/early spring and place the container in good light, out of direct sunlight. Do not let the room temperature exceed 15°C/59°F and water moderately. If the bulbs are to be planted outside after flowering, cut off the dead flowerheads and let the foliage die down naturally. Remove the corms and store in a cool dark place until the following autumn.

PROPAGATION Remove offsets from bulbs after flowering and set outdoors in drills or pots of soil-based compost. They should reach flowering size in 2 years.

VARIETIES 'Pickwick', lilac, striped purple; 'Purpureus Grandiflorus', rich purple; 'Joan of Arc', white; 'Dutch Yellow', bright golden yellow.

POSSIBLE PROBLEMS Generally trouble-free, but corms in storage may rot or be attacked by aphids.

▧ CARE TIP

Following flowering in pots indoors, the foliage should be left on the plants to die back naturally. When purchasing bulbs for pots select only top quality.

HIPPEASTRUM

spring	45cm/18in	bright	10°C/50°F	low

Hippeastrums are sometimes incorrectly sold as amaryllis, another bulbous species to which they are related. While several species are known, the most popular types for indoor decoration are named hybrids which produce their spectacular lily-like flowers of red, pink or white in early spring.

GENERAL CARE Pot up newly obtained hippeastrums in a soil-based compost. Half of the bulb should stand clear of the mixture. Keep just moist until growth appears. When the flower bud appears, bring the pot into good light and gradually increase the amount of water until, when the plant is in full flower, the compost is constantly moist. Some direct sunlight every day is essential, but the temperature should not exceed 18°C/65°F. After flowering gradually decrease watering but start feeding with liquid fertilizer every 2 weeks. Good light is still important. By late summer the dried foliage can be removed and the dormant period begins. Keep the bulb in its pot, dry, and keep at 10°C/50°F until the cycle begins again. Do not repot, but replace the compost every 3 or 4 years in early spring.

PROPAGATION Remove offsets when renewing the compost and pot them up in 7.5cm/3in pots.

VARIETIES *Hippeastrum* 'Apple Blossom', white streaked pink; 'Candy Cane', cream; 'American Express', scarlet.

POSSIBLE PROBLEMS Generally trouble-free.

▪ CARE TIP

Following flowering, the flower stem should be left to die naturally and the plant should be fed to build up the bulb. During its dormant autumn period the bulb should be stored warm and dry and brought into normal growing conditions towards the end of winter. Flowers normally appear before the leaves, and may be encouraged if the bulb is kept very warm during this period.

HYACINTH

spring	30cm/12in	bright	7°C/45°F	low

Hyacinths are sold in the autumn for spring flowering, or as bulbs specially prepared to bloom in the middle of winter. The most common form is the so-called Dutch hyacinth, which bears fragrant flowerspikes of white, pink, blue or yellow.

GENERAL CARE Pot up bulbs singly or several to a container close together but not touching, with the nose of the bulbs exposed. Use bulb fibre if the container has no drainage holes, otherwise a good soil-based compost. The compost should be evenly moist. Put the container in a cold, dark place; preferably outdoors, covered with a 15cm/6in layer of peat and a sheet of polythene. Check after 3 weeks to make sure the compost has not dried out. As soon as 5cm/2in of leaf can be seen, the pots can be moved into the light at a temperature of 10°C/50°F. As growth progresses the temperature may be raised to 18°C/64°F, no more. The bulbs cannot be used for indoor decoration again, but will grow in the garden. To prepare them, remove faded flowerspikes but not the stems or foliage, which should die down slowly in a cool place. Plant out in late spring.

PROPAGATION Bulbs for indoor forcing are raised by special techniques not recommended for amateurs.

VARIETIES *Hyacinthus orientalis* 'Blue Jacket' (*above*), 'Queen of the Blues'; 'Pink Pearl'; 'City of Haarlem', primrose yellow; 'Madame Sophie', double white.

POSSIBLE PROBLEMS Eelworms; aphids.

▪ GENERAL TIP

Placing three bulbs in bulb fibre to flower in bulb bowls in mid-winter can be very appealing. But it is essential that one should specify prepared bulbs when purchasing.

IRIS

| winter | 15cm/6in | bright | 7°C/45°F | low |

Several dwarf irises are suitable for growing in pots to bloom in winter or early spring. One of the most successful is *Iris reticulata*, a fragrant miniature in shades of purple and blue with orange 'beards'. If planted in late summer they bloom in the middle of winter; autumn-planted bulbs flower in spring.

GENERAL CARE Plant the bulbs 6 to a 12.5cm/5in half-pot containing a light soil-based compost, with plenty of drainage material in the bottom. Keep cool, just moist and shaded for about 8 weeks. When the leaves show, bring the pots into full light and a room temperature about 13°C/55°F. Remove faded flowerheads but let the foliage die down naturally and feed with liquid fertilizer every 4 weeks. After a dormant period the bulbs should flower again and will almost certainly do so if planted outside.

PROPAGATION Divide the bulbs and offsets after the foliage has died down and pot up. Small bulbils may take 2 or 3 years to reach maturity.

VARIETIES *I. r.* 'Cantab', pale blue; 'Harmony' (*above*), royal blue; 'J. S. Dijt', reddish purple.

POSSIBLE PROBLEMS Aphids; mould on badly stored bulbs.

PLANTING TIP

There are numerous miniature flowering irises, such as I. reticulata, that are pleasing in pots. Simply plant several to shallow pans and stand in the garden to bring in as flower buds appear.

NARCISSUS

| winter | 38cm/15in | bright | 7°C/45°F | low |

Types used for forcing into early growth indoors are derived from the species *Narcissus tazetta* (bunch-flowered narcissus) and hybrids with *N. poeticus* called poetaz narcissi.

GENERAL CARE Bulbs specially treated to bloom early should be planted in the autumn. Use bulb fibre if the containers have no drainage holes, otherwise any good peat-or soil-based compost. Set the bulbs in groups, sitting half out of the growing medium, which should be thoroughly moistened before planting. Keep very cool and preferably in the dark, for example, wrapped in black polythene and left outside. Inspect the pots occasionally to make sure the compost is not drying out. When about 7.5cm/3in of growth is visible, move the container into a well-lit position, preferably in direct sunlight. Keep the room temperature below 16°C/61°F or the buds will shrivel before breaking into flower. Discard the bulbs after flowering.

PROPAGATION Bulbs for winter forcing are raised by special techniques not recommended for amateurs.

VARIETIES Tazatta: 'Paper White' (*above*), delicate very pale cream petals. Poetaz: 'Cragford', white petals, deep red cup, 4-6 flowers per stem; 'Geranium', cream petals, orange cup, 5-6 flowers per stem; 'Silver Chimes', small, 9-10 very pretty blooms per stem, white petals, lemon cup.

POSSIBLE PROBLEMS Blindness – buds failing to open – occurs if the compost is not kept moist.

PLANTING TIP

A single layer of these bulbs in a pot can sometimes be disappointing. For fuller effect it is possible to use deeper containers and to introduce a layer of bulb fibre or potting soil, followed by closely placed bulbs, then more potting medium and a final layer of bulbs with finishing soil on top. The effect in the spring will be a double value display.

TULIPA

| winter | 38cm/15in | bright | 7°C/45°F | low |

Early-flowering tulips bring a splash of dramatic colour into winter displays. These species, which may bear single or double flowers, come in a breathtaking range of colours and combinations of colours (except blue). Both types have pointed, grey-green leaves. Like crocuses, only one variety should be placed in a pot, so that they will bloom together and achieve a pleasing uniformity of size.

GENERAL CARE Treat tulip bulbs exactly as narcissi. It is worth emphasizing that excessive room temperatures – over 16°C/61°F – will cause the flowers to fade quickly, while between 13 and 15°C/55 and 59°F they will bloom for up to 4 weeks. The bulbs cannot be used to flower indoors a second time, but if planted outside after the foliage has been allowed to die down naturally they may well flower for several seasons.

PROPAGATION Detach offsets, if any, from the bulbs after flowering and grow on in drills outside. They take 2-3 years to reach flowering size.

VARIETIES Single early, flowers pointed in bud, opening flat 7.5-12.5cm/3-5in across: 'Bellona', yellow; 'Pink Beauty', deep pink and white; 'Keizerskroon', yellow and red. Double early, peony-like flowers 10cm/4in across: 'Electra', pink-mauve; 'Wilhelm Kordes' orange and red; 'Peach Blossom', rose on white; 'Schoonord', white.

POSSIBLE PROBLEMS Mould on badly stored bulbs.

■ GENERAL TIP

Always plant individual varieties. Taller growing tulips are often unwieldy indoors, which may be a good reason for choosing some of the species that are compact in growth and very colourful.

VALLOTA

| summer | 45cm/18in | bright | 13°C/55°F | low |

Commonly known as Scarborough lilies, vallotas are related to hippeastrums. The two do look alike, but vallota flowers are only 10cm/4in across and the vallota blooms in summer. Up to 8 scarlet flowers are borne on a single erect stem.

GENERAL CARE Pot up in spring, one bulb to a 12.5cm/5in pot. Pack moist soil-based compost tightly around the bulb, so that half of it is visible above the surface. Place in good light at normal room temperatures. Water sparingly for 2 months then increase the amount of water to keep the compost just moist. At this point start giving a liquid feed every 2 weeks. When flowering is over substitute a high-potash fertilizer. Keep the plant in full light until the winter rest period, when indirect light will suffice. Water very sparingly and cease feeding during this time. Do not repot annually but top-dress (*see p.14*) with fresh mixture to which a little bonemeal has been added.

PROPAGATION When the pot becomes overcrowded with offsets and the original bulb has naturally divided into 3 or 4, separate them out gently and repot in the recommended mixture. This is best done in spring. Use 7.5cm/3in pots for small offsets and pot on the next year.

VARIETIES *Vallota speciosa* (*above*) is the only species available, with red flowers. Varieties include *V. s. alba*, white; *V. s. delicata*, salmon pink; *V. s. elata*, smaller with cherry-red flowers.

POSSIBLE PROBLEMS Mealy bugs on leaves.

■ CARE TIP

Like almost all of the South African flowering bulbs these are plants that enjoy a bake in the sun during their dormant period, and good light at all times while in growth. Cool indoor conditions will suit them fine as they are hardy in sheltered areas if planted fairly deep at the base of a sunny wall. This is an old favourite that deserves to be more popular.

CACTI

These are plants that are indigenous to the American continent, where the vast majority grow in arid, desert regions. Many attain great age and a size that is totally out of keeping with the small plants that one may grow on the windowsill at home. However, it is the latter that we are concerned with here – the sort of plants that are grown for room decoration, or in the greenhouse if one has the facilities and sufficient interest in the subject. The greenhouse, offering modest winter warmth and maximum light, is the best location for the sun lovers, but that is not to say that the kitchen windowsill does not produce its quota of quality plants.

PURCHASING

There was a time when only a few specialist growers offered cacti for sale, but things have changed and they are now on offer at a wide assortment of retail establishments. The specialist growers still exist, many of them operating on a very large scale that allows them to offer plants of surprisingly good quality throughout the year. Cacti are available in tiny pots or as giant specimens that will give the chosen site an instant desert ambience if there is a little sand about to complete the scene. Even the smallest of the purchased plants will be in the region of 3 years old, so will be well rooted in their pots when acquired. In spite of the wide variety that is generally available it will be difficult to locate some of the less popular plants. If you cannot find the plant you want, contact specialist growers direct – they will usually be found at one of the many flower shows that are held in the spring and summer months.

LOCATION

The general rule in this respect, with but a few exceptions, is that cacti must have the lightest location

available, and this will mean full sun in an arid atmosphere. In poor light the majority of plants become thin and etiolated with the result that they lose the tight, compact shape that is so important to their general appearance. Indoors, they should have a sunny window location. The tougher kinds can stand out of doors in good light during the summer, but care is needed to prevent their becoming too wet when it rains.

CONDITIONS

Dank and airless conditions can be fatal, so a light and airy atmosphere should be the aim. Although cacti are from desert regions the growing temperature should not necessarily be excessively high. In the desert the temperature can drop to a very low level at night, but cacti can tolerate these conditions as long as they are not wet at their roots; high temperatures will not be a problem, but if temperatures are to be below 5°C/41°F care is needed to ensure that the soil is dry.

WATERING AND FEEDING

Cactus plants that are permanently wet will have a very short life. Free-draining potting mixture is essential – a mixture that allows water to drain immediately through when it is poured on to the surface of the soil. During the spring and summer plants should be watered and allowed to dry before being watered again. During the winter months they should have no water whatsoever – this condition encourages flowering when water is given in the spring.

Fertilizers specially formulated for cactus can be bought, but a tomato fertilizer will usually do equally well. In general, one should feed established plants about once every 2-3 weeks during the spring and summer for the best possible results.

Cacti and other succulents can make a fascinating display. There are hundreds of species and varieties, many of which produce beautiful flowers.

POTTING AND POTTING MIXTURES

Mixtures formulated for cactus plants can be bought, and this is the best option for the beginner. When you have gained experience in the growing of these plants you can contemplate preparing your own concoctions, but it is not wise to experiment at the outset. All peat mixtures, or soil-less mixtures as they are termed, are unsuitable for cactus plants. It is much better to get a loam-based mixture – if it does not feel gritty when run through the fingers, additional grit or sharp sand should be added to improve the drainage. Never use potting soil that has been standing around unused for long periods of time. Plants should be repotted in the spring or early summer and should be well provided with roots; poorly rooted plants should be returned to the pot in which they are growing. When potting on 'spiteful' plants it may be necessary to put a paper collar around the plant to make handling easier.

PESTS AND DISEASES

Cactus plants are not too much troubled by either pests or diseases, but overwatering may well cause the fungal problem of botrytis which is seen as a blackish wet mould around the base of the plant. Treating with a fungicide might well save the plant, but it is doubtful. Affected plants should be isolated from others in the collection.

Mealy bug is the biggest problem, and these insects are normally detected as a waxy cotton-wool-like substance nestling between the leaves and stems of plants. The adult bugs look like powdery white woodlice which can be clearly seen as they move about, and will not be difficult to eradicate. The young of this pest are ensconced in the waxy wool and are much more difficult to make contact with. One way is to use an old toothbrush that has been soaked in methylated spirits to wipe them off the plant; this will also see off the adults.

Mealy root bug is often quite easy to see. The young are wrapped in a cottony coating resembling cotton wool and they leave a white deposit on the inside of the container – when detected immerse the pot to its rim in insecticide to eradicate. Always follow insecticide directions and wear rubber gloves.

APORACACTUS FLAGELLIFORMIS

2m/6ft 6 in	trailing	direct sun	5°C/41°F	dry

Native to Mexico, *Aporocactus flagelliformis* (rat's tail cactus) can be grown as trailing plants in a basket, or as creeping plants in a large cactus garden.

GENERAL CARE When spring potting on is required use a peat or loam-based mixture and never allow the soil to dry out, keeping just moist over the winter months. While in active growth, spring and summer, feed fortnightly with a tomato fertilizer.

PROPAGATION Remove mature lengths of growth in early summer and allow to dry for a day or two before inserting in peat and sand mixture.

SPECIES *A. mallisonii*, pendulous spiny stems and large flowers, rarely found on sale.

POSSIBLE PROBLEMS Mealy bug and root mealy bug; treat the latter with a solution of Malathion insecticide by watering it into the soil, giving sufficient to see surplus draining through the holes in the bottom of the container. Mealy bug in the foliage should be treated with a systemic insecticide. Wear rubber gloves and apply out of doors.

CEPHALOCEREUS SENILIS

90cm/3ft	upright growth	direct sun	7°C/45°F	dry

Of Mexican origin, *Cephalocereus senilis* (old man cactus) will attain a height of some 12m/39ft in their native habitat, by which time they will be of considerable age. With roots confined to plant pots growth is very slow.

GENERAL CARE Provide the warmest possible position and very good light. Over the winter months the soil should be quite dry, but during the spring and summer it should be watered and allowed to dry out before repeating. When potting on, use a very open mixture containing a good proportion of grit.

PROPAGATION In late spring/early summer the top section of the stem may be removed and propagated in peat and sand mixture, but this does ruin the appearance of the plant. Allow the severed end to dry over a period of days before inserting.

SPECIES *C. sartorianus*, *C. chysacanthus*, both with upright columns of growth.

POSSIBLE PROBLEMS Mealy bugs and root mealy bug; treat with insecticide as soon as detected.

■ DESIGN TIP

These are excellent plants for suspending from a high ceiling near a window that offers good light, but it is important to check watering regularly during the summer months to ensure that the soil is not becoming too dry.

The cerise-coloured flowers, which each last for several days, are an added bonus and are produced in some quantity.

■ CARE TIP

The long grey hairs of old man cactus will become tarnished in time, and may be cleaned by giving the plant a shampoo with a mild solution of detergent.

CEREUS PERUVIANUS

2m/6ft 6in pot grown	columnar	direct sun	5°C/41°F	dry

The erect habit of this easy-care plant, known as blue column, adds much to the cactus collection. The botanical name suggests that it is indigenous to Peru, but this is, in fact, a plant that is widely used in South America and there is doubt concerning its true origin.

GENERAL CARE Offer good light at all times and keep the soil dry over the winter. In spring and summer, water and allow to dry before repeating. Use clay pots and a free-draining mixture when potting on – avoid getting the plant pot-bound.

PROPAGATION Large sections of the stem of overgrown plants can be cut, allowed to dry and propagated in cactus mixture.

VARIETIES Numerous, but naming is confused unless plants are obtained from a reliable source.

POSSIBLE PROBLEMS Generally trouble-free, but there is always the possibility of root mealy bug – easily detected when the plant is removed from its container.

CHAMAECEREUS SILVESTRII

low growing clumps	neat mounds	sunny	0°C/32°F	dry

These accommodating little plants are colloquially known as peanut cactus. They must be almost everyone's introduction to the growing of cacti, as they are readily available, easy to grow and almost every little piece that breaks off will make excellent propagating material.

GENERAL CARE A high temperature is not needed, but if the temperature is unavoidably very low the soil must be kept dry. When potting use shallow pans as opposed to full-depth pots and employ a well-drained cactus mixture. Keep dry over the winter months.

PROPAGATION Growth resembles tiny green sausages and almost any piece that is detached will root readily in any reasonable mixture.

VARIETIES *Chamaecereus silvestrii*, bright scarlet flowers; *C. s.* 'Orange Hybrid', orange flowers.

POSSIBLE PROBLEMS The most likely cause of failure is that of having the soil in the pot much too wet when the prevailing temperature is very low.

■ CARE TIP

These are vigorous plants that will develop bold and spiteful columns of growth that are probably best suited to the greenhouse or large conservatory. They overbalance very easily so heavier clay pots are an important requirement when potting plants on – a task that should not be neglected. Moving larger plants is a two-handed task that needs care.

■ PROPAGATION TIP

Young children can be shown how to remove the little sausages of growth carefully with a pair of tweezers so that they can propagate their own plants.

CLEISTOCACTUS STRAUSII

2m/6ft 6in	columnar	direct sun	5°C/41°F	dry

The common name 'silver torch' is very apt as the slender columns of growth are generously provided with white spines along their entire length, giving the plants a pleasing silvery appearance when seen in good light. Bolivia is generally credited with being the place of origin.

GENERAL CARE Because of their eventual height it is wise to use heavier clay containers when plants are being potted on. Use a loam-based, free-draining mixture and pot on in spring. Plants are reasonably vigorous in growth so potting on should not be neglected. In spring and summer feed with tomato fertilizer and keep moist, but keep dry in winter.

PROPAGATION Cut stems and allow them to dry before inserting in peat and sand mixture.

VARIETIES *Cleistocactus strausii juyjuyensis*, *C. baumannii* and *C. smaragdiflorus* may occasionally be available. A feature of these plants is erect, spiny stems.

POSSIBLE PROBLEMS Generally trouble-free, but watch for mealy bug.

ECHINOCACTUS GRUSONII

60cm/24in	90cm/3ft	full sun	7°C/45°F	dry

Native to Mexico and the aristocrat among cacti, *Echinocactus grusonii* (golden barrel) is seen at its best when very mature and developed into a huge globe of bristling yellow spines.

GENERAL CARE Best suited to shallow terracotta containers and a porous cactus mixture, golden barrel should be potted on in the spring, but only when it is necessary as a result of root development. Provide a dry atmosphere and sun and at all costs avoid dank and airless conditions. Water well and allow to dry before repeating. Keep dry over winter months.

PROPAGATION From seed collected from plants growing in the wild, but rarely available.

SPECIES *E. grandis* and *E. texensis* are available , but *E. grusonii* is the best choice.

POSSIBLE PROBLEMS Mealy bug and root mealy bug; cold and wet conditions present the greatest difficulty, hence the need for controlled temperatures in winter.

▤ DESIGN TIP

Silver torch is one of the most attractive of cacti when seen in a group with other varieties, and it is generally better when forming part of a small collection rather than when used as a solitary specimen. Grouping of cacti is an exercise seen to best effect when plants are grown in the greenhouse or the conservatory where there is greater space available.

▤ CARE TIP

Large specimens of E. grusonii will become the cactus grower's prize possession and must, consequently, be handled with great care. When potting or moving make it a two-handed task.

ECHINOCEREUS

30cm/12in	compact clumps	full sun	5°C/41°F	dry

There are numerous varieties of these interesting plants, commonly known as lace and hedgehog cactus, mainly originating from the southern states of America and Mexico. A major benefit is that they produce flowers with little difficulty at an early age. Even without flowers the plants are attractive in appearance, some forming clumps of growth early on, whereas others take time for their true habit to establish.

GENERAL CARE To do well plants need the lightest possible location and the growing medium must be free-draining – add extra sand to the chosen potting mixture. It is important to allow the mixture to dry out between waterings.

PROPAGATION Cut mature pieces of stem and allow to dry before inserting.

SPECIES *Echinocereus viridiflorus, E. rigidissimus* and *E. fitchii*; large pink flowers are freely produced.

POSSIBLE PROBLEMS Mealy bug and root bug are the most likely pests to be found.

FEROCACTUS

compact	15cm/6in	direct sun	5°C/41°F	dry

These become very large and very vicious plants in their natural habitat, but when pot-grown can be contained within acceptable dimensions. They do not produce flowers as pot plants until they have attained reasonable size. Their common name is 'fire barrel'.

GENERAL CARE These plants must have very good light in which to grow and at no time should the potting mixture become too wet – add extra sand or grit to the potting mixture when repotting in spring. Water and allow the soil to dry well before repeating.

PROPAGATION Ferocactus can be propagated from seed if available.

SPECIES *Ferocactus acanthodes* is the most popular, but *F. herrae (above), F. horridus* or *F. latispinus* may also be available.

POSSIBLE PROBLEMS Mealy bug or root mealy bug. Wet roots through poor culture will be fatal.

▓ FLOWERING TIP

Although these are plants that will flower naturally at an early age it is important to offer the right conditions – a very long and very dry winter season, followed by spring watering to encourage flowering.

▓ CARE TIP

This plant is also known as the fish-hook cactus and fish-hook barrel on account of its vicious hooked spines; handle it with the utmost care!

GYMNOCALYCIUM

| 10cm/4in | 7.5cm/3in | full sun | 5°C/41°F | dry |

These are lovely plants that form neat clumps of growth in a reasonably short space of time, and they will also oblige with attractive flowers while still of tender age. There are numerous varieties available and all of them are delightful plants for the cactus enthusiast. The common name is 'spider cactus'.

GENERAL CARE Like most cactus gymnocalycium must have free drainage and any purchased potting mixture should have additional sand incorporated to improve its porosity. Watering can be fairly generous while the plants are in active growth, when they will also benefit from an application of tomato fertilizer every 2 weeks or so.

PROPAGATION Thin out congested clumps carefully, using a narrow-bladed knife, and insert the thinnings in a peat and sand mixture to produce new plants.

SPECIES *Gymnocalycium venturianum (above)*, *G. bruchii*, *G. horridispinum*, *G. quehlianum* are among the many varieties. All are easy to care for.

POSSIBLE PROBLEMS Mealy bug, root mealy bug.

LOBIVIA

| 15cm/6in | clump forming | direct sun | 5°C/41°F | dry |

A pleasing characteristic of the lobivias (cob cactus) is their ability to flower at an early age, and the fact that flowers come in a range of colours.

GENERAL CARE Plants must be kept dry over the winter months, but it is important not to allow the soil to become excessively dry during the growing season. Pot on, if necessary, in spring – add sand to standard potting mixes to improve the drainage factor. Following potting on the soil should be well watered and thereafter kept on the dry side to encourage root development in the new mixture. Apply tomato fertilizer in the growing season to encourage flowering.

PROPAGATION From offsets allowed to dry before inserting in a peat and sand mixture in early summer. These should be kept in good light but out of bright sun until they have rooted.

SPECIES *Lobivia maximiliana*, *L. aurea*, *L. bruchii*, *L. famatimensis*, among others; most are indigenous to Argentina. Deeply ribbed growth – normally little trouble to flower.

POSSIBLE PROBLEMS Root mealy bug and mealy bug – careful inspection is needed to detect latter.

CARE TIP

Gymnocalycium 'Hibotan' is much used for grafting on to stronger-growing stock, so a red, pink, yellow or even white gymnocalycium can be purchased perched on top of its host plant. It is important when overwintering such plants to maintain a minimum temperature of 10°C/50°F, as cold winter conditions can prove fatal.

PLANTING TIP

In shallow terracotta pans, lobivias make fine specimen plants when well matured. Preparation of these takes some time in the potting from one size of container to the next, so patience is needed!

MAMMILARIA

| varied | varied | direct sun | 5°C/41°F | dry |

Almost all species of this greatly varied genus are indigenous to Mexico, and there are many excellent plants among them. The majority are easy-care plants that will not only grow well but will also flower well at an early stage in their development. Most form tight clumps of attractive colouring and can be encouraged to form into specimen plants in shallow containers in time.

GENERAL CARE Offer good light at all times and keep dry over winter to encourage flowering when water is again applied in early spring. Established plants will benefit from a weak solution of tomato fertilizer during the growing season.

PROPAGATION The majority are propagated from detached offsets. It is also possible to propagate from seed.

SPECIES *Mammilaria bocasans, M. backbergii, M. elongata, M. zeilmanniana (above)*, plus many others that will enhance any cactus collection.

POSSIBLE PROBLEMS Root mealy bug and mealy bug – the latter may be difficult to detect among the clustered offsets.

NOTOCACTUS

| 10cm/4in | 7.5cm/3in | full sun | 5°C/41°F | dry |

Notocactus (ball cactus) are fine plants of attractive shape, mostly globular but some becoming columnar as they age. Spines and colouring are generally very attractive, and there is the added bonus that plants are not difficult to bring into flower. They are indigenous to tropical South America.

GENERAL CARE Provide good light for all notocactus and ensure that they are growing in a free-draining potting mixture by adding grit or sand to commercially prepared mixtures. Water with care during the growing season and feed occasionally. No winter watering is needed.

PROPAGATION From seed or offsets where available.

SPECIES *Notocactus horstii, N. herterii, N. ottonis; N. leninghausii* is particularly attractive, developing a stout column 25cm/10in tall with pale yellow spines.

POSSIBLE PROBLEMS The most common pests are mealy bug and root mealy bug. When detected both should be attended to without delay.

■ GENERAL TIP

An added interest for the keen cactus grower is to concentrate on one type of plant in particular (mammillarias, for example) and to become something of a specialist grower of these plants.

■ CARE TIP

Plants that form tight clusters of rosettes provide the perfect hiding place for mealy bug with the result that these pests often go unnoticed until they have become well established. Pick up the plants periodically and give them a closer inspection so that mealy bug can be controlled at an early stage of development.

OPUNTIA

1.8m/6ft	1.3m/4½ft	direct sun	5°C/41°F	dry

'Bunnies' ears' is the perfect plant for children if they mind their fingers, and it is one of the most popular cacti of all. Some of the opuntias (prickly pear) have clusters of small bristle spines while others have vicious barbs, so all must be handled with some care. Most are easy to manage with the more robust, *O. robusta* for example, being very vigorous and needing to be reduced in size periodically – use trimmings for propagation. Opuntias are indigenous to the southern United States and tropical South America.

GENERAL CARE All need good light and dry winter conditions, but should be kept moist and fed during the growing season.

PROPAGATION From seed or from trimmings – allow to dry before inserting in peat and sand mixture.

SPECIES *Opuntia microdasys* (bunnies' ears, *above*), *O. leucotricha*, *O. tuna* plus many others.

POSSIBLE PROBLEMS Check frequently for mealy bug and root mealy bug.

PARODIA

7.5cm/3in	7.5-20cm/3-8in	full sun	5°C/41°F	dry

Indigenous to Argentina, parodias (Tom Thumb) have become much more popular in recent years – much of the popularity being due to their willingness to flower as young plants. They are mostly of globular shape, with vicious hooked spines.

GENERAL CARE Over-wet conditions will cause rotting so water must be given with care. For the same reason plants must not be potted in containers that are too large – it is better to have smaller pots that allow the soil to dry more readily. Good light and free-draining soil mixture are important requirements. A sunny location will also help to alleviate damp conditions.

PROPAGATION From seed or offsets. Seed, when obtainable, should be sown in shallow seed pans filled with a proprietary seed sowing mixture to which grit or sand has been added.

SPECIES *Parodia chrysacthioa* (*above*), *P. aureispina*, *P. microsperma*, *P. sanguiniflora*, *P. mutablis*; all globular in shape and free-flowering.

POSSIBLE PROBLEMS Mealy bug and root mealy bug.

■ CARE TIP

Some of the opuntias will tolerate much lower temperatures than that indicated above if they are kept very dry. However, it is better to offer modest warmth.

■ FLOWERING TIP

Parodias have the considerable bonus as far as cactus are concerned in that they are able to produce their large red and yellow flowers at an early age. Given a reasonable collection of these plants one may have flowers over an extended period during the spring and summer months of the year.

PERESKIA

9m/30ft	climber	direct sun	13°C/55°F	dry

A cactus plant because of its barbs, but a most unlikely-looking candidate to be included in the family *Cactaceae* as the leaves are smooth and the plant is seen at its best when treated as a climbing subject. If grown in a pot indoors it can be trained on a light trellis placed in the pot, or if grown in the greenhouse it can be trained on a wall support. Its common name is 'Barbados gooseberry'.

GENERAL CARE Keep moist and feed occasionally during the spring and summer, but exercise care over winter as plants are susceptible to a combination of cold and wet.

PROPAGATION From cuttings in spring – place in small pots filled with a peat and sand mixture and root at a temperature of 21°C/70°F.

SPECIES *Pereskia grandiflora* (above), *P. rubescens*, *P. aculeata* 'Godseffiana'; the latter offers pale gold foliage and is the most widely available.

POSSIBLE PROBLEMS Mealy bug and root mealy bug.

REBUTIA

7.5cm/3in	7.5cm/3in	full sun	5°C/41°F	dry

The rebutias (crown cactus) have become very popular plants in recent years for the simple reason that they are small and easy to accommodate and that they flower very freely as young plants. There is a wide colour range of bright flowers. They are native to Argentina and neighbouring countries.

GENERAL CARE Plants must have a long winter rest from watering – from mid September to mid March. Begin watering again when flower buds are seen to be forming. Grow in small pots in good light and avoid overwatering. From the time of bud formation plants can be fed at fortnightly intervals with a tomato fertilizer.

PROPAGATION From seed or from offsets.

SPECIES *Rebutia pygmaea, R. senilis, R. deminuta* among others. Large numbers are grown from seed, so it might be difficult to obtain true named varieties.

POSSIBLE PROBLEMS Mealy bug and root mealy bug.

▓ FLOWERING TIP

Grow a single strong shoot attached to a cane and when strong enough use as a stock for grafting epiphyllum or zygocactus to the top to set them off more effectively when in flower.

▓ CARE TIP

These are ideal plants for the living-room windowsill as they occupy little space and, if offered good light, can almost be guaranteed to flower each year from an early age. When curtains are drawn in winter plants should be brought into the room rather than being left on a cold windowsill.

SUCCULENTS

These are different from the cacti in that they do not have areoles, a small cluster of spines that are found only on members of the family *Cactaceae*. Succulents belong to many different families of plants, but they do have one thing in common – their swollen stems or leaves are capable of holding moisture and nutrients to enable plants to survive long periods of drought in their natural habitats. In desert regions of the world these plants can withstand the most arid conditions with the capacity to burst into brilliantly coloured flower almost as soon as the first rains of the new season find their way to the roots of the plants.

This gives some indication of the watering requirements of these plants. In the UK, the winter represents the dry season and both cacti and succulents should have little or no water from about the end of September through to the early spring, when watering will induce many of the freer-flowering plants to produce their blooms.

LOCATION

Succulents are almost all sun-lovers, so the lightest possible location should be chosen for them, both indoors and in the greenhouse. In the home, plants ought to have a sunny windowsill, and where space is limited it may be possible to have narrow shelves at a higher level to accommodate smaller plants. High-level window shelves of this kind are frequently seen on the Continent, where the growing of all kinds of indoor plants seems to have reached almost the stage of obsession in some households! Such shelves need not be elaborate and can be supported on either side by appropriate fittings on the window frame.

CONDITIONS

The majority of succulents will tolerate temperatures around freezing point and will not be unduly harmed as long as the soil in the growing container is dry. However, it is generally better to offer plants a temperature of 10°C/50°F over the winter months, with higher temperatures tending to be beneficial rather than harmful. In most homes some rooms are warmer than others over the winter and if there are a number of plants they should be gathered together and placed in the warmest room so that they may benefit from the better conditions.

When these plants are grown as isolated decorative features in a room the tendency is to put the pots into decorative outer containers. A word of warning here – you must put a good thickness of pebbles in the bottom of the container before introducing the plant so that water draining from the growing pot will filter away into the gravel.

WATERING AND FEEDING

Dry winter conditions are essential – if plant roots are wet over winter and the temperature is low there is every chance that the plant will succumb. When it comes to caring for succulents (and cacti) there is a misguided belief that they need no attention other than the occasional drop of water. This is far from true, as will be seen from a visit to a succulent collection that is receiving proper care in respect of watering, feeding, potting on, suitable temperature and good light. Freshly potted plants should not be fed, but those that are established will benefit from feeding about every second week during the spring and summer months when growth is active. In terms of suitability and economy there is nothing better than a tomato fertilizer – it will not only benefit the plant generally, it will also encourage those that do flower to flower more freely.

POTTING AND POTTING MIXTURES

Established plants should be potted on in the spring to containers that are only slightly larger than the one in which the plant is growing. Specially prepared mixtures for cacti and succulents can be bought and this is probably the best option where only a few plants are concerned. In any event, it is most essential that the mixture should be free to drain, and that means that as you pour water on to the surface of the soil it should immediately soak away. To improve porosity of any mixture that is suspect you can add sharp sand, coarse grit or perlite.

CONTAINERS

There are all sorts of containers available and it does not seem to make a great deal of difference whether they are terracotta or plastic. However, to have a collection of plants in a hotch-potch of containers of different materials, sizes and colours tends to mar the overall appearance. Complete standardization is seldom possible but there should be a degree of uniformity, even if it means nothing more than having all plastic containers of similar colour.

PESTS AND DISEASES

Prevention is better than cure, which means that plants ought to be regularly inspected for the presence of pests such as mealy bug, which is the one most commonly found in succulents. These pests get into the most inaccessible places and their presence is only made known when a waxy substance rather like cotton wool is seen amongst the branches and leaves of plants.

A collection of succulents grown in a dish container look good with textured small rocks and stones.

AEONIUM

1.5m/5ft	compact growth	good light	5°C/41°F	dry

The most common of these is *Aeonium arboreum*, which is available with dark bronze or fresh green leaves. Both form strong stems from which rosettes develop. Indigenous to the Mediterranean region, aeonium require lots of sunshine and reasonably dry conditions in which to grow. As time goes on they will develop into quite substantial plants that look good growing in terracotta planters on a sunny patio. *A. domesticum Var.* has much softer rosettes of growth that do well on a sunny windowsill indoors.

GENERAL CARE Keep moist during the summer months and very much on the dry side at other times. Feed occasionally while in active growth.

PROPAGATION By mature offsets in free-draining mixture. Keep out of bright sunlight until they have rooted.

SPECIES *A. arboreum (above)*, green form; *A. arboreum atropurpureum*, bronze form; *A. domesticum Var.*; pale green and cream rosettes; *A. urbicum*, large rosettes, yellow flowers.

POSSIBLE PROBLEMS Mealy bug, but not greatly troubled.

AGAVE AMERICANA

6ft 6in	6ft 6in	good light	5°C/41°F	dry

Both height and spread will vary depending on location – in a container they will be much less, while planted out in a greenhouse the plant will be larger. The best location is probably a sunny patio in a terracotta container. The leaf tips are viciously pointed, so plants must be out of the way and care must be taken when inspecting them. In spite of these problems, *Agave americana* (century plant) is a magnificent plant when grown as a specimen. The large rosettes of leaves are an attractive grey and cream in colour.

GENERAL CARE Offer good light and never overwater. When container-grown, plants should be in a heavier loam-based potting mixture as opposed to a peaty concoction.

PROPAGATION From maturing offsets taken from around the base of the plant. Leave to dry for several days before potting in a potting compost.

VARIETIES There are many varieties available.

POSSIBLE PROBLEMS Generally trouble-free.

▩ PLANTING TIP

A. domesticum var. is a splendid plant for growing indoors if it has a light location. Rosettes of softish growth develop on firm stems to provide a very attractive plant. Worth seeking out.

▩ FLOWERING TIP

The century plant is seen growing in all tropical parts of the world where it develops into a plant of considerable size. Although it may take up to 10 years, plants do produce flowers and when they arrive they do so in style by attaining a height of up to 12m/40ft. Following flowering it is not unusual for plants to die.

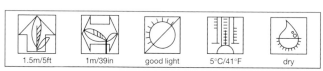

ALOE

1.5m/5ft	1m/39in	good light	5°C/41°F	dry

Aloe variegata has a tight, spiralling rosette of leaves that are green with paler bands of colour, which gives the plant its common name of Partridge Breast Aloe. It is a very easy windowsill plant to manage. The Medicine Aloe, *A. Vera*, is much more rambling and untidy with appreciably larger rosettes of growth. The latter lives up to its common name in that the sap from a broken leaf has amazing curative qualities when rubbed on to burns or bruises – a plant that is worth having for this reason if for no other.

GENERAL CARE Aloe needs a light location. Keep plants moist during the spring and summer and on the dry side at other times. Feed occasionally with a tomato type fertilizer.

PROPAGATION Propagate from offsets; insert in sandy mixture to start them off.

VARIETIES There are numerous varieties, all rosette forming.

POSSIBLE PROBLEMS Occasionally mealy bug, but not greatly troubled.

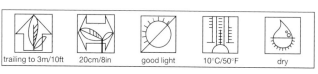

CEROPEGIA

trailing to 3m/10ft	20cm/8in	good light	10°C/50°F	dry

Ceropegia is sometimes called rosary vine, but the heart-shaped leaves frequently get in a tangle, giving it the more commonly used name 'hearts entangled'. It is essentially a hanging container plant, be it in a conventional basket or decorative pot. The leaves are attached to very slender stems that will trail for yards if the container is suspended at reasonable height. The mauve-coloured tubular flowers are interesting, as are the peculiar round growths that appear on the stems of older plants. These can be used for propagating new plants.

GENERAL CARE These are very tolerant plants that put up with all sorts of varying conditions – their pet hate being a combination of wet soil and low temperatures.

PROPAGATION From cuttings or stem growths. Cuttings should go into peat and sand mixture, several cuttings to each small pot. A heated propagator will assist rooting.

SPECIES *Ceropegia woodii* (*above*), heart-shaped leaves, insignificant flowers.

◾ GENERAL TIP

While A. variegata is an excellent windowsill plant for the home, it is better to grow A. vera in the greenhouse to form clumps and to propagate single rosettes for a handy position on the windowsill.

◾ PROPAGATION TIP

When planting decorative hanging pots put at least 10 rooted cuttings into the soil and when these have reached manageable size peg them down in the soil to provide additional growth.

COTYLEDON

60cm/24in	erect habit	good light	10°C/50°F	dry

These South African succulents have particularly attractive foliage – not only do the leaves have a scallop-shell appearance, but they are also covered in an attractive mealy bloom. The stems of the plant also have similar covering which adds much to the general appearance.

GENERAL CARE Plants must have good light in which to grow and at no time should the soil be too wet – best practice is to water adequately and then to allow the soil to dry appreciably before repeating. A weak tomato fertilizer at fortnightly intervals in spring and summer will encourage growth. Sharp, well-drained potting mixture is important – the sort of mixture that allows water to drain through as soon as it is poured on to the surface of the soil.

PROPAGATION From seed or from cuttings.

SPECIES *Cotyledon elegans* (*above*), *C. undulata*, attractive grey foliage with undulating leaf margins.

POSSIBLE PROBLEMS Mealy bug and root mealy bug. Check for root mealy bug by removing the plant from its pot – white deposit on the pot confirms its presence. Eradicate by immersing the pot in malathion insecticide – wear rubber gloves and soak thoroughly.

CRASSULA

1m/39in	60cm/24in	good light	5°C/41°F	dry

In recent years the money plant (or jade plant) has become very popular. There is a green form and an excellent variegated form in *Crassula argentea* 'Hummels Variety', both of which have thick, strong stems on stout plants if not mollycoddled.

GENERAL CARE Keep in good light, avoid overwatering, restrict to modest-sized pots and feed every 10 days in spring and summer. Pinch out growing tips frequently early on so that compact and solid-looking plants develop. When potting on as plants of mature size use clay pots and a loam-based potting mixture.

PROPAGATION From cuttings – allow the severed end to dry before inserting in growing compost.

SPECIES *C. argentea*, *C. a.* 'Hummels Variety', *C. corymbulosa* (*above*).

POSSIBLE PROBLEMS Generally trouble-free.

◾ CARE TIP

The decorative mealy covering on the leaves can be very easily damaged through use of unsuitable insecticides. Check suitability first, or experiment with smaller plant first by treating it and leaving for a time before applying insecticide generally.

◾ CARE TIP

It is important to grow these in the manner that the professional would describe as 'hard', which means no high temperatures and little fussing. Plants can be outside all the time while the weather is not very cold.

E CHEVERIA

Variable	compact rosettes	good light	10°C/50°F	dry

These are among the most attractive of foliage plants, having many superb metallic shades of colour. By way of a bonus they will generally not be difficult to bring into flower. The majority form neat rosettes of growth that make it possible for a large collection to be fitted into a reasonably small space.

GENERAL CARE Care is needed to ensure that water does not lie in amongst the overlapping leaves of rosettes, and that watering in general is done with care, particularly during the winter months of the year. Use a free-draining mixture when plants are being potted on, and feed with a tomato fertilizer every 2-3 weeks during spring and summer.

PROPAGATION From offsets that form around the base of the parent rosette.

SPECIES *Echeveria derenbergii* (*above*), orange flowers; *E. hoveyii, E. setosa*, red flowers.

POSSIBLE PROBLEMS Mealy bug and root mealy bug.

E UPHORBIA

2m/5ft 8in	varied	good light	10°C/50°F	dry

There are many plants in this large family, all of them producing a milky sap when bruised or cut. Some resemble cacti and carry spines.

GENERAL CARE Plants should be dry from the end of the summer until the spring when watering for the new season can begin, but it must at no time be excessive. For this reason it is essential to employ a free-draining potting mixture when plants are being potted on. Avoid the use of shallow pans as plants are deep rooting.

PROPAGATION From seed, or cuttings where available.

SPECIES *Euphorbia obesa* (*above*), *E. melaformis, E. ingens* (giant form).

POSSIBLE PROBLEMS Generally trouble-free, but check for mealy bug.

■ CARE TIP

Allowing dead and dying leaves to remain on plants can cause the entire plant to rot and die. Check base of rosettes for discoloured leaves regularly and remove. Blemished leaves are nothing more than an eyesore, so should be removed during regular inspections. The most common reason for loss of leaves is wet and cold winter conditions.

■ PROPAGATION TIP

To propagate from seed you will need to have both male and female plants in your collection. The seed pods explode when ripe, scattering seeds widely, so place some muslin over the plant before the seeds ripen.

GASTERIA

squat	squat	filtered light	5°C/41°F	dry

Gasteria are unusual in succulents in that these are plants preferring light shade as opposed to the sunny conditions that are normally needed. Grown from seed, gasterias will in time form attractive rosettes of growth but this takes some time to develop as plants will initially have a central stem from which leaves develop opposite to one another. Being shade tolerant, the gasterias make fine house plants that have the added advantage of being very compact so occupying little space.

GENERAL CARE A free-draining potting mixture is essential. Gasterias will need more frequent watering than the majority of succulent plants but it is necessary to allow the soil to dry out between each application. Reduce the watering over the winter months.

PROPAGATION From seed, or from offsets for true varieties.

SPECIES *Gasteria batesiana*, *G. maculata*, *G. verrucosa* (*above*).

POSSIBLE PROBLEMS Generally trouble-free.

KALANCHOE

1m/39in	upright growth	good light	10°C/50°F	dry

There are numerous kalanchoes available that will add interest to a plant collection but none, perhaps, more pleasing than *Kalanchoe tomentosa* (*above*). The common name is Pussy Ears doubtless gained from the leaves, which are covered with fine silver hairs and edged with a rich brown colour.

GENERAL CARE Grow in full sun; water sparingly, especially in winter. Feed once every two weeks during the active growth period. Kalanchoes are no trouble to care for – they should be renewed when they become overgrown and ungainly.

SPECIES Other interesting species include *K. daigremontianum*, *K. tubiflorum*.

POSSIBLE PROBLEMS Generally trouble-free.

▮ DESIGN TIP

One of the great pleasures of growing both succulents and cacti is to produce symmetrical plants of good dimension. The gasterias lend themselves well to this purpose, looking especially well in shallow pans. Pans planted with a single mature rosetting plant can be very effective if properly dressed with gravel on the soil surface to set off the plant.

▮ FLOWERING TIP

The kalanchoe is a short-day plant, which means that it only develops flower buds when the day lasts for less than 12 hours. You can replicate these conditions at home by creating artificially dark conditions using a black plastic bag or bucket. Start the treatment in late summer and continue for between 12 and 15 weeks – removing the first few flower buds to promote flowering.

KALANCHOE BLOSSFELDIANA

| 1m/39in | sprawls if uncontrolled | good light | 10°C/50°F | dry |

The most popular of all succulents, this plant is available in flower all year round as a result of growers manipulating the amount of light that is available to the plant. Long-lasting flowers in several colours are an attraction for many weeks. An excellent use for this fine kalanchoe is to group several in a shallow dish to provide a more impressive room feature. These are also good plants for edging decorative plant borders within the conservatory. They are commonly known as 'flaming Katie'.

GENERAL CARE Offer good light, modest warmth and pot on after flowering to produce bright and vigorous plants. Avoid overwatering, feed occasionally while in active growth and regularly remove dead flowers to keep plants in good fettle.

PROPAGATION Top sections of stem with a few leaves attached will root readily in peat and sand mixture.

VARIETIES Red, yellow, orange and pink-flowered varieties are available.

POSSIBLE PROBLEMS Generally trouble-free.

LITHOPS

| 2.5cm/1in | very compact | full sun | 5°C/41°F | dry |

Fascinating succulent plants from South Africa, lithops (living stones) are almost guaranteed to capture the interest of younger members of the family.

GENERAL CARE A bright, sunny location is essential to their well-being, as is careful watering. Ensure that no water gets on to the plants and during the winter months do not water at all as dry soil conditions are essential during this time. There should be no hurry to apply water in the spring – allow plants to remain dry until the growth of the previous year has shrivelled away and fresh growth is evident. This will normally be in late spring. Water plants thoroughly but allow the soil to dry before repeating. Free-draining soil is needed when potting plants on.

PROPAGATION From seed, or by splitting older clumps during the summer months.

SPECIES There are many species, but plants are frequently sold as unnamed seedlings.

POSSIBLE PROBLEMS Generally trouble-free.

■ FLOWERING TIP

This kalanchoe often fails through lack of attention following flowering. After flowering the dead flowers should all be removed and plants should be potted into larger containers to grow and prosper.

■ PLANTING TIP

Because living stones take up little space they can be grouped together in a shallow terracotta pan along with a selection of pebbles – this will be something of a tease for anyone trying to identify the actual plants.

PACHYPHYTUM

30cm/12in	30cm/12in	good light	5°C/41°F	dry

With rounded, fleshy leaves, these are very much one's impression of what a succulent should be. Besides a pleasing shape, the leaves have the added benefits of being subtly coloured with an overall mealy covering. Rosettes of leaves form on long stalks that can be staked to remain erect or can be allowed to spread naturally to give a more pleasing appearance.

GENERAL CARE Water and feed occasionally during the spring and summer, giving no feed and only minimal watering over the winter months. Avoid getting water on to the foliage and be especially careful when using insecticides – malathion, for example, can be harmful. Use loam-based, free-draining potting mixture when potting on.

PROPAGATION From rosettes cut off and dried at severed ends before inserting in sandy potting mixture.

SPECIES *Pachyphytum bracteosum, P. longifolium, P. oviferum (above)*, all having very colourful fleshy foliage.

POSSIBLE PROBLEMS Mealy bug and root mealy bug.

SEDUM MORGANIANUM

trails 60cm/24in	trailing	good light	10°C/50°F	dry

Sedum morganianum (burrows tail) can only be grown as a trailing subject, having pendulous stems that are densely covered with overlapping succulent leaves that give the plant its very distinctive appearance. Older plants will in time produce clusters of pink flowers, but the foliage is the main attraction of this interesting plant.

GENERAL CARE Initially they should be grown in pots to establish; once well-developed a group of 5-6 plants should be planted into a hanging basket of good size (a large size is needed because it will be almost impossible to remove the plant to pot into a larger basket once it has become established as a trailer). Keep moist and in good light.

PROPAGATION Propagates very readily from leaves, which will break off and root of their own accord.

VARIETIES There are no varieties.

POSSIBLE PROBLEMS Generally trouble-free.

■ CARE TIP

The attractive mealy covering on the leaves is a principal attraction and it is necessary to grow these plants in full sun so that the mealiness and general colouring is enhanced. When handling plants with this sort of covering it is important not to touch the leaves, and when watering one should do so with care, directing the water into the pot and not over the foliage.

■ CARE TIP

One of the greatest difficulties with this plant is that it will shed leaves at almost the slightest touch. Since it has dense foliage a few leaves are not missed, but care in handling is important.

SENECIO ROWLEYANUS

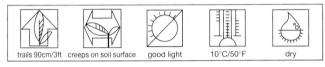

trails 90cm/3ft	creeps on soil surface	good light	10°C/50°F	dry

With the fashion for trailing plants indoors this senecio has become very popular. The pendulous slender stems with green bobbles of leaves will, if grown in a greenhouse, eventually reach the staging or floor where they will root in and spread naturally in all directions. The common name is 'string of beads'.

GENERAL CARE Plants should be kept moist during the summer and only just moist over the winter. Feed occasionally in summer. When growing these plants indoors, as opposed to a greenhouse, they should be given the lightest possible location – hanging close by the kitchen window being ideal.

PROPAGATION Fresh plants can easily be made by severing rooted pieces from the main stem and potting them in a free-draining mixture.

VARIETIES there are no varieties.

POSSIBLE PROBLEMS Generally trouble-free.

STAPELIA

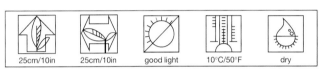

25cm/10in	25cm/10in	good light	10°C/50°F	dry

The stapelias (carrion flowers) have attractive succulent stems borne in clusters forming at soil level. They are quite easy to grow, but you may prefer to have them in the greenhouse rather than indoors – certainly while they are in flower, because the flowers have an abominable odour that has the very uncharming feature of attracting blowflies that help to pollinate the flowers. Nevertheless, the star-shaped flowers have fascinating patterns and colouring which might well outweigh the unpleasant smell that they produce.

GENERAL CARE Stapelias should be grown in a very sharp compost and should at no time be excessively watered. The latter is particularly important over the winter months.

PROPAGATION By removing mature stems and potting in small pots during the summer. If done with care it is possible to remove stems that already have roots attached.

SPECIES *Stapelia hirsuta, S. revoluta, S. variegata (above)*, all have attractive flowers with an unpleasant odour.

POSSIBLE PROBLEMS Mealy bug and botrytis rot.

▓ DESIGN TIP

This senecio is seen to best advantage when growing in small hanging containers – the appearance of the hanging unit can be enhanced by placing it in a wicker hanging container. As with many such hanging plants the senecio will become rather sparse around soil level. To compensate for this, root a few cuttings and plant them in the soil.

▓ CARE TIP

Stapelias have a tendency to rot off at the base of their stems – a problem that is aggravated by wet conditions. Allow the soil to dry between waterings and cover the surface with a layer of gravel for added protection.

103

BROMELIADS

The bromeliads are a large family of plants from tropical America, a small number of which are popular for indoor decoration. They owe their name to a seventeenth-century Swedish botanist, O. Bromel. Bromeliads are distinguished in appearance by their stiff, spiky leaves, which are almost always stemless,

and which form densely packed rosettes. The flowers may nestle in the cup of the rosette, emerge from closely packed bracts at the tip of a flowerstem, or droop from the end of it. The cup or 'vase' at the centre of the rosette in some genera collects a reservoir of water to supply the plant's needs. In most other plants, other than those that live in ponds, the constant presence of water at the heart would cause rot and ultimately death. In nature, most of the bromeliads grown as houseplants are epiphytic, that is they grow on another plant, often a tree, but take no nourishment from it (they are not parasites, in other words). They can do this because their roots are adapted to thrive without soil. While the roots can absorb moisture and nourishment from the air, very little moisture is lost through the strong leaves. Commonly called air plants, epiphytic bromeliads thrive where the atmosphere is humid and the temperature uniformly high. Terrestrial bromeliads grow in the ground.

With the exception of cryptanthus, bromeliads bear showy, colourful flowers, often surrounded by pink or red bracts. Some are borne on long flower spikes. Others have almost no stem at all and at flowering time the leaves or leaf bases surrounding the vase from which the bloom emerges change colour, taking on a gorgeous deep red hue. In nature this would attract pollinating insects and birds.

SPECIAL CARE

Despite their exotic appearance and unique characteristics, bromeliads are not difficult to grow indoors as long as a few basic requirements are met. Their adaptability is shown by the fact that bromeliads in the wild growing on the branches of a tree sometimes fall off and simply continue growing on the ground. For houseplants, the growing medium should be porous and completely free of lime. Suitable mixtures are (a)

Stripes or prominent bands are features of the earth star. Good light gives best colouring.

equal parts of peat and coarse leaf mould with half a part of coarse sand for improved drainage; or (b) equal parts of peat, sand and osmunda fibre or (c) equal parts of leaf mould, sphagnum moss and peat. Since the roots obtain relatively little nourishment from the mixture, pots as small as 12.5cm/5in are large enough; but because roots provide anchorage, the pots should be relatively heavy. Clay pots rather than plastic ones are recommended.

An intolerance of lime means that water used to fill the vases and spray the leaves should be either rainwater, the ideal choice, melted ice from a defrosting refrigerator (let it reach room temperature before use) or tap water, if unavoidable, which has been boiled and allowed to cool. The central vase, in plants which have one, should be full of water at all times. Replace it about every four weeks, turning the plant upside down to let the stale water drain away. Stand bromeliads outside in warm summer showers; the rain provides nourishment while washing the leaves. Indoors, maintain humidity at steady, reasonably high levels with the temperature between 16–18°C/61–64°F and in good light (see below). Many bromeliads do not have a natural rest period, but if it is not possible to maintain these conditions through the year they will survive the winter quite happily as long as the temperature does not drop below the minimum given in each entry – with a corresponding lessening of humidity. Requirements for light differ between those which have tough leathery leaves and can take a certain amount of direct sunlight, and those with softer, finer foliage which in nature would thrive in dappled light. For these, bright filtered light is best.

'Like a specimen tree on a manicured lawn, bromeliads invite individual attention. In a heated greenhouse or conservatory, they may be expected to co-operate in a larger display, but in a room setting they look best situated as one might a prize piece of china, enjoying pride of place on a table or pedestal. Having said that, the unique growing habits of bromeliads make it possible to combine a number of different species in a single setting, namely a bromeliad tree (see below).

PROPAGATION

Aechmea and billbergia, in particular, produce several offsets from each plant, and you can have four or five new plants from one parent. When bromeliads have flowered, the central rosette begins to die, but the offsets which have been produced around it will continue to grow. Treat them like the parent plant until they are at least 15cm/6in high and are ready to be detached. The best time to do this is in summer. Knock the whole plant from its pot and ease away the growing mixture. Pull away each offset, complete with its roots, taking care not to damage them. Pot up singly in 7.5cm/3in pots of moist compost. Sit the base of the plant on the surface, covering the roots. Do not bury the crown. Top up the vase with water, if there is one, and keep shaded until well-established. Young plants should have a resting period from late autumn to early spring. Although the leaves of the parent will remain handsome for several months, it will not flower again and should be discarded.

MAKING A BROMELIAD TREE

An artificial home for bromeliads can be formed from a seasoned branch cut from a hardwood tree, such as apple, although this will tend to rot in time. A very effective substitute can be made from pieces of cork bark fixed to a suitable support. This looks good and is long-lasting. Secure the trunk end of the 'tree' in a small tub or some other container, such as a stone trough, with a wide base and firm bottom. The size of the branch very much depends on the area in which the bromeliad tree will be positioned, but in proportion to the size of the plants a branch 1.2–1.8m/4–6ft is best.

One of the best ways of securing the branch is to place the end in the container, and to pour cement around it. Shingle or small stones can then be placed over the concrete.

Set the individual plants in the crevices of the branch; these can be found by pouring water down the branch and seeing where it naturally collects. Remove the plants from their pots and wrap the root-balls in sphagnum moss. Mould the moss around the roots so that it is firmly fixed to them. Put the plants in place and use green plastic-coated wire to hold each soil-ball together and also to attach it securely to the branch. Water the soil balls thoroughly and spray them regularly to prevent them drying out. Eventually the roots will bind themselves to the tree and the wires can be removed.

AECHMEA

| 60cm/24in | 60cm/24in | bright | 10°C/50°F | high |

Aechmeas produce long-lasting blooms that vary in appearance from species to species. All invariably have beautifully marked, curving strap-shaped leaves in rosette formation.

GENERAL CARE By nature epiphytic, in the home aechmeas may be grown in 15cm/6in pots of any of the recommended mixtures (*see p.105*). Keep the central vase filled with rainwater or cooled boiled water during the summer, replacing it with fresh water every 8-12 weeks. Keep the compost just moist throughout the year. Feed with liquid fertilizer every 4 weeks in summer, either by adding it to the vase or with a foliar spray. Maintain high levels of humidity by misting around the plant. Keep in full sun at a temperature in the range 16-18°C/61-64°F. A brief drop in temperature will do no lasting harm, especially if the compost is barely moist. If repotting is necessary, do so when new growth begins and use clay pots for stability.

PROPAGATION Detach rosettes when they are one-third to half the size of the parent plant and place in 5cm/2in pots of the standard compost. Keep in good light and just moist until well established.

SPECIES *Aechmea fasciata* (urn plant, *above*), green leaves banded silver, flowers blue in bud opening to rose pink, summer; *A. fulgens*, 38cm/15in high, broad green leaves, waxy blue flowers followed by scarlet berries.

POSSIBLE PROBLEMS Generally trouble-free.

■ GENERAL TIP

The brush-like pink bract of this plant is colourful for many weeks. When no longer attractive it should be cut away, by which time one or more young growths will be evident at the base of the stem. Avoid damaging these as *they can be cut away when large enough and potted individually in an open, free-draining medium to flower in, perhaps, two to three years.*

ANANAS

| 90cm/3ft | 90cm/3ft | bright | 10°C/50°F | high |

The ananas family includes the edible pineapple as well as several highly decorative species suitable as house plants. They are slow-growing terrestrial bromeliads with arching spiny leaves in rosette formation. Mature plants produce 7.5cm/3in long blue flowers which are followed by distinctive pineapple-shaped fruits.

GENERAL CARE Grow in a mixture of 2 parts loam, 1 part leaf-mould or peat and 1 part sand. Ananas do not need a resting period, and should be sited in full sunlight all year. Temperatures in the range 16-18°C/61-64°F are ideal, though lower temperatures can be tolerated in winter. Give a feed of liquid fertilizer every 2 weeks throughout the year. Keep the compost constantly moist with rainwater or cooled boiled water and spray the foliage regularly with a fine mist. Repot young plants annually in spring until they reach 20cm/8in pots. Use clay pots for stability.

PROPAGATION Remove offsets with a sharp knife when about 15cm/6in long and pot up in a moistened peat and sand mixture.

SPECIES *Ananas comosus* (pineapple), edible fruits not produced in the home. *A. c.* 'Variegata' (*above*) has leaves edged yellow, tinged rose pink in good light; *A. nanus*, only 45cm/18in high with very graceful leaves, produces a fragrant green (inedible) fruit and numerous offsets.

POSSIBLE PROBLEMS Generally trouble-free.

■ GENERAL TIP

Spectacular plants at any time when mature, but much enhanced in appearance as the pineapple fruit begins to develop and the plant colouring becomes suffused with reddish pink hues.

BILLBERGIA

| 45cm/18in | 60cm/24in | bright | 2°C/35°F | low |

Billbergia nutans (*above*), popularly known as angel's tears or queen's tears, is one of the prettiest bromeliads and one of the easiest to grow. Its long, strap-like leaves arch over in an attractively random fashion, and the pendent flowers – which usually appear in late spring – are tinged blue, yellow, pink and green, encased in pink sheaths.

GENERAL CARE Grow this terrestrial plant in small clay pots (12.5cm/5in) containing any of the recommended mixtures (*see p.105*). As there is no need for a rest period, water the compost moderately all year using rainwater or cooled boiled water and give a liquid feed every 2 weeks, either into the pot or as a foliar spray. Normal room temperatures are suitable, but very low temperatures are well-tolerated for short periods. Stand the plants in good light, out of direct sunlight. Repot young specimens in spring.

PROPAGATION Detach offsets when they are half the size of the parent plant. Let the cut surface dry for 24 hours before potting up in one of the recommended mixtures.

HYBRIDS *B.* × 'Windii', a hybrid of *B. nutans* with stiff, grey-green leaves, blue-green flower petals reflexed to reveal long creamy stamens.

POSSIBLE PROBLEMS Generally trouble-free.

CRYPTANTHUS

| 30cm/12in | 38cm/15in | bright | 10°C/50°F | moderate |

The many forms of cryptanthus or earth star have a tendency to hybridize easily, giving rise to an amazing variety of multi-coloured specimens. It is their unusual foliage for which they are prized, as the flowers are usually hidden by the abundant leaves, which grow in rosette form.

GENERAL CARE Cryptanthus are terrestrial bromeliads. Grow in small pots or half-pots of peat-based compost kept constantly moist during the growing season. When resting give just enough water to prevent the compost drying out completely. Very little feeding is required, perhaps 2 applications of a liquid fertilizer in summer. Bright light is important to maintain leaf colour. Normal room temperatures are suitable: above 18°C/64°F ensure humidity by placing the pots on trays of moist pebbles. Repot only when the pot is crowded with offsets.

PROPAGATION Detach offsets in spring and pot up in small pots of peat and sand.

SPECIES *Cryptanthus bromelioides tricolor* (rainbow star, *above*), wavy mid-green leaves striped white, tinged pink in good light, produces plantlets at the end of stolons rather than offsets; *C. zonatus*, spreading habit, wavy leaves striped olive and silvery green.

POSSIBLE PROBLEMS Generally trouble-free.

▓ DESIGN TIP

A much underrated easy-care plant that is seen to best effect when growing in a hanging container that will show off the pendulous bracts to full advantage. Whereas the majority of plants in elevated positions might suffer as a result of arid conditions the billbergias are much more tolerant. Small hanging pots can be plunged to give them a good soak.

▓ DESIGN TIP

The Earth Stars are composed, in the main, of tight clusters of rosettes that make these plants the perfect residents for bottle gardens and terrariums where compact growth is essential.

NEOREGELIA

30cm/12in	60cm/24in	bright	16°C/61°F	moderate

The foliage is very beautiful, long, strap-like leaves arching outwards in a perfect rosette with a vase at the centre. Gorgeous reds and pinks tint the leaves for some months during the flowering period, though the flowers are insignificant.

GENERAL CARE By nature epiphytic, neoregelias have no clearly defined rest period. Grow in clay pots no larger than 12.5cm/5in containing a mixture of equal parts of sand, leafmould and loam, kept nicely moist all year. Use rainwater or cooled boiled water and keep the vase filled with water too, draining and replacing it every 4 weeks. Give a liquid feed at half-strength every 2 weeks to the compost, the vase and as a foliar spray. Stand in bright light, with some direct sunlight every day. Mist over with a fine spray to maintain humidity. Repot small plants in spring if necessary.

PROPAGATION Stolons are produced at the base of the plants. When they have formed roots of their own, carefully detach them from the parent, preferably in spring, and pot up in small pots of the recommended mixture.

SPECIES *Neoregelia carolinae*, bright green, long pointed leaves flushed red or purple at flowering time. 'Tricolor' (*above*) is a variety with leaves striped white. The whole plant turns rose red at flowering time; *N. spectabilis* (fingernail plant), leathery dark green leaves tipped bright red.

POSSIBLE PROBLEMS Generally trouble-free.

■ CARE TIP

As with most bromeliads this is one of the toughest plants for growing indoors, so it is well suited for more difficult locations that offer reasonable warmth and light. Plants will be much better if the central urn is kept filled with water and only minimal watering is the aim in respect of the compost in the pot. The potting mix should be very open.

NIDULARIUM

30-40cm/12-18in	45cm/18in	bright	13°C/55°F	high

Nidulariums resemble neoregelias in that they produce a rosette of glossy green leaves which acquire a pink tinge at the centre during the flowering period. The leaves are rather broader, however, and have spiny edges. Flowering only occurs in mature plants, after which they slowly decline, to be replaced by offsets produced in the leaf axils.

GENERAL CARE By nature epiphytic, nidulariums should be grown in clay pots no larger than 10cm/4in containing one of the recommended mixtures (*see p.105*). As there is no defined rest period, water moderately all year using rainwater or cooled boiled water. Feed with liquid fertilizer at half-strength every 2 weeks. Keep the vase filled with water, draining and replacing it every 6 weeks. Stand the pots in bright, filtered light at normal room temperatures. To keep the level of humidity high, stand the pots in saucers of moist pebbles. Repot in spring if necessary.

PROPAGATION Offsets are produced at the base of the plant, very close to the parent. When they have acquired the characteristic rosette shape, remove them carefully, leave to dry for 1-2 days and pot up in the standard mixture.

SPECIES *Nidularium fulgens* (*above*), shiny, arching, fresh green leaves spotted darker green, bright red central inflorescence; *N. innocentii*, green leaves tinged reddish-brown, white flowers surrounded by orange bracts.

POSSIBLE PROBLEMS Generally trouble-free.

■ GENERAL TIP

Another of the cart-wheel type bromeliads with leaves radiating from a short central trunk. When significant flowers appear, the main rosette will begin to deteriorate before dying.

TILLANDSIA

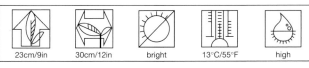

23cm/9in	30cm/12in	bright	13°C/55°F	high

Tillandsias are epiphytic bromeliads with a negligible root system. They can be grown on a bromeliad tree (*see p.105*) where they will absorb most of their food supply through their leaves, or they can be set in small pots. The grassy, arching leaves are attractive, but it is chiefly for their extraordinary inflorescence that tillandsias are grown. These blooms may appear at any time from late spring until late autumn. They consist of tightly overlapping pinkish bracts arranged in a flat, pointed oval, from which 1 or 2 small, bright purple flowers emerge.

GENERAL CARE Pot up in one of the recommended mixtures (*see p.105*). Keep the compost just moist but spray the leaves every other day. Set the pots in saucers of moist pebbles. Every 4 weeks, apply a little liquid fertilizer at half-strength. Tillandsias need bright, filtered light, and temperatures about 16°C/61°F. Repotting should not be necessary.

PROPAGATION Detach the small offsets and pot up in 7.5cm/3in pots in a peat/sand mixture.

SPECIES *Tillandsia cyanea* (*above*), narrow rosette of smooth green leaves striped brown, pink-purple inflorescence on short stem; *T. lindeniana*, 50cm/20in high, dark green leaves, purple beneath, 15cm/6in flower spike of pink bracts with blue flowers.

POSSIBLE PROBLEMS Generally trouble-free.

▮ GENERAL TIP

These have achieved tremendous popularity in recent years under their common name of Air Plants, which alludes to the fact that many of them virtually survive on what is blowing about or contained in the atmosphere.

You see them in all sorts of stores, often attached to anchorages with an adhesive. But it is better to buy plants with their roots growing in pots.

VRIESIA

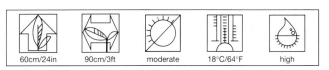

60cm/24in	90cm/3ft	moderate	18°C/64°F	high

Vriesias of various species are found all over Central and South America. They are impressive plants which require a stable environment to give of their best. All types produce handsome leaves in a perfect rosette with a central vase for retaining water. Mature plants produce erect, dramatic flower spikes.

GENERAL CARE Grow in 12.5cm/5in pots containing a mixture of sand and leaf-mould, loosely packed around the roots. In spring and summer water by filling the vase with rainwater or cooled boiled water, allowing it to spill over and moisten the compost. Every 4 weeks, feed with liquid fertilizer at half-strength. In winter, give enough water to keep the compost just moist. Normal temperatures are suitable, but bright filtered light is essential. To maintain high levels of humidity, place the pots in saucers of moist pebbles. Repot only if the roots fill the pots.

PROPAGATION Detach offsets bearing roots from the base of the plants when they are half the size of the parent. Allow to dry for 1-2 days then pot up in the recommended mixture.

SPECIES *Vriesia hieroglyphica* (king of bromeliads, *above*), wide, acid-green leaves irregularly banded purplish-brown, yellow flower in spring on erect, 75cm/2½ft stem; *V. splendens* (flaming sword), leaves banded green and brown, 60cm/24in flower stem bears a 30cm/12in scarlet inflorescence from which yellow flowers appear in late summer.

POSSIBLE PROBLEMS Generally trouble-free.

▮ GENERAL TIP

The larger species, such as V. fenestralis, are very difficult to acquire and would be much too large for the average room. Upright rosettes have spectacular flowers that last well.

ORCHIDS

Interest in these fascinating plants is clearly on the increase as more and more people find cut flowers in a local department store, or maybe even on a petrol station forecourt. Orchids in these places will almost certainly have been flown in from the Far East, where orchid farms cover vast acreages to provide cut flowers for virtually the entire world.

Some of the better garden centres stock a range of pot plants throughout the year, and this could well be the best initial source of supply. You may be able to purchase priced-down plants that have finished flowering but will be fine for the future if they are still in good condition. You can also order plants from such a garden centre, but as your interest increases you will want to acquire a list of orchid plant suppliers so that you can contact the grower direct.

LOCATION

The majority of orchids are epiphytic, meaning that they use other plants as hosts – often trees growing to considerable height. They do not take any nourishment from the tree, relying on what is available in the atmosphere for food and water. Consequently, you should provide a light and airy location. Indoors, this will mean having plants near a window as opposed to in a dark corner that is devoid of light, with little in the way of air circulation. If there is insufficient natural light in the room, you can grow many orchids very successfully under strip lights. Ordinary warm white fluorescent tubes will do, provided they are suspended at a reasonable distance from the plant material.

You may want to provide a plant window – a bit like a bay window, but with the extension going further out from the house to provide a comfortable area for plants. A sliding glass window can isolate this area from the rest of the room so that the plant window can be individually provided with heating, lighting and whatever else might be thought necessary.

CONDITIONS

Humidity is a key factor in the cultivation of most orchids and humid conditions can only be achieved by a combination of warmth and moisture. As far as temperature goes there are three distinct groups of orchids; cool growers (minimum temperature 10°C/50°F), intermediate growers (minimum temperature 13°C/55°F) and those needing a higher temperature of 18°C/65°F. When you buy plants you should make it clear to the supplier the sort of temperature you can maintain so that warm-loving plants are not acquired for conditions that are inadequate. It is also necessary to offer plants fresh air on warmer days of the year.

WATERING AND FEEDING

Plants should be kept moist at all times while they are actively growing, with a little less water needed while they are inactive. In the greenhouse it is necessary to perform the operation of damping down regularly in order to maintain humidity levels – much more important in summer than winter. Indoors, plants should be provided with trays containing a moisture-retaining material, such as gravel or Leca granules. In hot weather plants will benefit from misting of the foliage. Electrically-operated humidifiers are available.

Orchid fertilizers are available and these should be used as directed – plants normally require feeding during the spring and summer months.

POTTING AND POTTING MIXTURES

Because orchids are epiphytic, it is essential that any potting medium is as open and free-draining as possible. This means that almost all of the standard potting mixtures are unsuitable. Until you have had plenty of experience of growing orchids it is best to select an orchid potting mixture that has been specially prepared for these plants.

In general terms, the best time to pot orchids on into larger containers is the spring, with the summer months being the least suitable. Avoid the temptation to pot plants on for the sake of it – small plants in very large pots rarely do well, be they orchids or any other plant.

CONTAINERS

There is a wide range of containers you can use – not least the humble polypropylene pot that is available in many shapes and colours (although the majority of plants do better when grown in black pots). You can buy a special orchid pot made of polypropylene with open sides to provide maximum aeration. You may be fortunate enough to acquire clay orchid pots, even clay pots with pretty patterned holes in their sides, but you may have to visit a Far East orchid farm to obtain supplies! Many orchids will also grow happily on slatted wooden rafts or in square hanging containers that are made from slatted laths. Where there is high humidity and regular attention plants can be grown epiphytically by attaching them to sections of cork bark, or simply to well-soaked sections of timber. The inventive indoor gardener can devise all sorts of ways of displaying and growing his or her plants to full advantage.

PESTS AND DISEASES

Orchids have their problems in full measure with red spider mites, aphids, mealy bugs, scale insects, fungal diseases, viruses and, for full measure, petal blight.

A wonderful showy display of white orchid blossom enhances the neutral colour scheme of this interior.

ANGRAECUM

60cm/24in	45cm/18in	good light/summer shade	18°C/65°F	high

Angraecum are indigenous to tropical Africa. The flowers are greenish white in colour, some fragrant, with a distinctive spur that may be all of 30cm/12in long. Plants are seen at their best when growing on a raft or in lath basket that offers maximum aeration to the roots.

GENERAL CARE Angraecum are reasonably easy to care for if the minimum temperature can be maintained. Offer good light but shade from very strong sun and ensure a moist atmosphere at all times. Keep moist throughout the year and feed regularly while the plant is in active growth. Mist leaves frequently.

PROPAGATION Scandent species by severing stem below the aerial roots and allowing growth to show before removing and potting up.

SPECIES There are several species but only *Angraecum sesquipedale* (*above*) is likely to be available; it has creamy white fragrant flowers.

POSSIBLE PROBLEMS Generally trouble-free.

CATTLEYA

50cm/20in	40cm/16in	filtered sun	10°C/50°F	high

Cattleya (green orchid) are from tropical South America and are among the most desirable of orchid plants..

GENERAL CARE Watering can be a critical factor, and the best advice is never to be too generous. If the general area can be kept moist the plant will absorb moisture from the atmosphere, so needing less direct watering into its container. Feed with a weak fertilizer solution every 2 weeks, alternating with a foliar feed at every third feeding application. Offer good light but protect from sun. Potting on of established plants should be done in the spring. Put drainage material in the pot and use porous potting mixture.

PROPAGATION Divide mature clumps; the section for propagating should have at least four pseudobulbs to be successful.

SPECIES There are many species and varieties available. 'Pink Debutante' (*above*), *C. skinnerii, C. bowringiana* will give a good start, offering large exotic flowers..

POSSIBLE PROBLEMS Slugs on young shoots; thrips on opening flowers; scale insects and mealy bug.

■ CARE TIP

Indoors, only the miniature forms are suitable and these should be grown in an enclosed plant case. To economize in the greenhouse it is wise to section off a small area that can be kept warmer for the more demanding plants. Given moisture and temperature the angraecums are not difficult to grow.

■ CARE TIP

With pests, prevention is better than cure and immediate remedial action should be taken when pests are suspected as it is much easier to eradicate a few than an infestation.

COELOGYNE

| 35cm/14in | 50cm/20in | filtered summer/bright winter | 10°C/50°F | moist |

Coelogyne are indigenous to South-east Asia. They may produce upright or hanging flower spikes, and fragrance may be an added bonus. The smaller species may be grown successfully indoors but some species can become very large in time, needing ample growing space. Small plants should be grown in pans, larger plants in pots of suitable size and pendulous plants are best in hanging containers.

GENERAL CARE Plants require a dry winter rest with watering starting again when fresh growth is evident early in the year. Some species require higher growing temperature than that indicated above, so ascertain plant needs when purchasing.

PROPAGATION Divide plants when repotting in the spring.

SPECIES *Coelogyne ochracea*, *C. cristata*, 'Chadwort' (*above*), *C. corymbosa*; all reasonably easy to care for.

POSSIBLE PROBLEMS Slugs, aphids, mealy bug.

CYMBIDIUM

| 1.5m/5ft | 1m/39in | good light | 10°C/50°F | airy |

Indigenous to South-east Asia, these are among the most spectacular of orchids. They are reasonably easy to manage indoors, bold groups being especially suited to a roomy conservatory. During the summer they can have a sheltered location out of doors.

GENERAL CARE Airy and cool conditions are essential during the summer months if plants are to bloom over the ensuing winter. Plants subjected to low temperature during the winter months will be very shy of flowering, so it is important to get the balance right. Cymbidium are evergreen and need no rest period.

PROPAGATION From seed (a specialized task) or by dividing mature plants.

SPECIES There is a very extensive range with highly coloured flowers.

POSSIBLE PROBLEMS Red spider mites, scale insect, mealy bug and others. Hygiene and regular inspection are essential.

■ PLANTING TIP

The coelogynes are epiphytic in their habit, meaning that they generally grow naturally in elevated locations, such as trees. The more pendulous types may be attached to trees in the greenhouse, but where space is limited a slatted hanging container will be more manageable. These should be lined with sphagnum moss before introducing potting mixture and the plant.

■ PROPAGATION TIP

Cymbidium are ideal beginners' plants as they flower freely and are reasonably easy to manage. They are also easily propagated. Healthy plants will quickly fill their containers with pseudobulbs; following flowering a sharp knife can be used to divide the bulbs for propagating. Select two bulbs, one with a shoot, and cut cleanly then pot into orchid potting mixture.

DENDROBIUM

| 2m/6ft 6in | upright growth | good light | 10°C/50°F | moist but airy |

Dendriobium is one of the largest groups in the orchid family, some of the varieties being deciduous, some semi-evergreen and some evergreen. They are grown in South-east Asia, where humidity and conditions in general are ideal, for export in their thousands to destinations in the west.

GENERAL CARE Provide dry and light winter conditions, but ensure that the soil is not excessively dry as this will cause the canes to shrivel. When flower buds appear in spring give a thorough watering and keep moist throughout the summer. When repotting is necessary do it when new growth is evident, using orchid potting mixture. Never overpot these plants.

PROPAGATION Plants may form plantlets with roots on the main stem; remove and pot up.

VARIETIES *Dendrobium nobile* (*above*) and a vast selection of species and varieties available.

POSSIBLE PROBLEMS Red spider mites – treat and repeat is the best advice. Use a recognized insecticide to control.

ENCYCLIA

| 45cm/18in | 30cm/20in | filtered light | 10°C/50°F | maintain low level |

These plants from tropical South America prefer cool conditions in which to grow, which makes them reasonably suitable as indoor plants as well as good subjects for a cooler greenhouse than the norm. Different varieties will flower at different times of the year, with *Encyclia cochleata* seeming to flower the year round when established. Fragrance is an added bonus.

GENERAL CARE These are plants that prefer to grow on the dry side regardless of the season and for this reason they do well when attached to sections of bark or board rather than being grown more conventionally in pots.

PROPAGATION Propagation can be done quite simply by dividing bulbs and potting them singly.

SPECIES *E. cochleata, E. citrina, E. mariae, E. nemorale* (*above*) *E. radiata*; all compact and reasonably easy to grow.

POSSIBLE PROBLEMS Check regularly for the presence of slugs, aphids and mealy bug. The use of a systemic insecticide can be very helpful in controlling aphids and mealy bugs.

■ CUT FLOWER TIP

A great benefit of the dendrobiums is their prolific flowering and their long-lasting qualities as cut flowers. If flowers have been removed from the plant for some time they should be immersed completely in water and left there to soak to extend their life when placed in the flower vase.

■ PLANTING TIP

Sections of cork bark can be purchased for attaching orchid plants to. Soak the bark, knock in a few nails at the back for ties and wrap plant roots in moss before fixing. Water by immersing.

MILTONIA

| 50cm/20in | 40cm/16in | good light | 13°C/55°F | dry atmosphere |

The miltonias (pansy orchids) produce flowers in numerous colours for many months of the year if one is fortunate enough to have a collection of plants. There are two distinct types – those originating in Brazil and those from Colombia. Many of the plants have pleasing fragrance and have the added bonus of flowering more often than the usual once in each year.

GENERAL CARE Miltonias need to be grown in warm conditions but not at excessive temperature. A winter rest is not needed so watering can continue throughout the year. Repot when the plants are showing signs of fresh growth. Use an open orchid mixture, but never repot unless it is necessary.

PROPAGATION By division of established clumps, or by removal of backbulbs.

SPECIES *Miltonia endressii*, 'Peach Blossom', *M. spectabilis*, offering an excellent colour range of attractive flowers.

POSSIBLE PROBLEMS Red spider mite.

OODONTOGLOSSUM

| 30cm/12in | 30cm/12in | shade from sun | 10°C/50°F | moist but airy |

Many Oodontoglossum (clown orchids) make excellent indoor plants that are not too difficult to care for, but check with the supplier that plants are suited to home conditions.

GENERAL CARE Moist atmosphere is important but it is also necessary to provide good air circulation, which may well mean having heaters in operation and ventilators open at the same time. Low-level vents are often better than those at higher level when plants are being grown in a greenhouse. Winter rest period should be checked with the supplier as winter care conditions vary with different plants.

SPECIES Numerous; *Oodontoglossum bictoniense* and *O. grande* (the attractive tiger orchid, *above*) are reasonably durable and easy to flower.

PROPAGATION By removal and potting of backbulbs from mature clumps. Large clumps provide the best flowers.

POSSIBLE PROBLEMS Aphids, mealy bug and red spider mite – control with malathion insecticide.

▧ CARE TIP

Being plants that are in growth throughout the year these are orchids that will need constant attention to ensure that they remain in good health. As with most established orchids they will require regular feeding once established in their pots. For simple, easy-to-use stimulant use a tomato fertilizer which is high in potash and will encourage production of flowers.

▧ PLANTING TIP

These are epiphytic plants so must have an open, free-draining potting mixture. Plants may be potted on at almost any time, but spring is favourable when new shoots are developing.

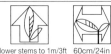

PAPHIOPEDILUM

| 40cm/16in | 40cm/16in | filtered light | 13°C/55°F | high |

Originating in South-east Asia and among the most popular of all orchids for indoor cultivation, the paphiopedilums (slipper orchids) are neat in habit, bearing erect flower stems with slipper flowers in many colours.

GENERAL CARE In a dry indoor atmosphere it is necessary to mist plants with water in warmer conditions. The controlled conditions of a plant-growing case are generally ideal for these easy-care plants. They should not be subjected to the bright light that may prevail on a sunny windowsill. Good air circulation is important in stuffy conditions – a fan may be necessary.

PROPAGATION By separating established clumps and potting severed smaller clumps individually in small pots.

VARIETIES There are many to choose from – when purchasing stipulate the easier kinds if you are a beginner.

POSSIBLE PROBLEMS Slugs and snails. Water in the centre of leaves can cause rotting.

PHALAENOPSIS

| flower stems to 1m/3ft | 60cm/24in | shade in spring/summer | 18°C/55°F | high |

Among the most rewarding of plants, all Phalaenopsis (moth orchids) need adequate temperature to succeed. Their individual arching stems produce a large number of spectacular long-lasting flowers, much used for floral displays. They originate from South-east Asia.

GENERAL CARE Shade from strong sunlight is essential during spring and summer, and at other times if very sunny. Offer high humidity and air circulation – electrically-powered fans are ideal for this purpose. Plants are evergreen and do not require winter rest so water, though reduced, must not be discontinued. Plants have no storage pseudobulbs so need regular feeding at intervals of 2-3 weeks.

PROPAGATION Difficult for the amateur grower – it is better to buy small plants for growing on.

SPECIES There are many species, among them *Phalaenopsis schilleriana*, *P. lueddemanniana*, *P. aphrodite*, with flowers said to resemble tropical moths flying in the night.

POSSIBLE PROBLEMS Check regularly for slugs and snails. Avoid getting water amongst the leaves.

▨ PLANTING TIP

Quite small plants are occasionally available and these should be carefully potted into small pots using a fine grade of bark. Potting on of small plants should be more frequent than for older plants. For older plants *choose a coarser grade of bark mixture – preferably a mixture specially prepared for orchids. The best time for potting older plants is while in active growth.*

▨ PLANTING TIP

Many of the phalaenopsis are propagated in culture flasks in laboratory conditions; pot these in very fine bark mixture. All potting should be done while growth is active.

PLEIONE FORMOSANA

| 30cm/12in | 30cm/12in | good | 4°C/39°F | cool and airy |

The alpine orchid, seen more frequently in a rock garden display rather than in an orchid house. These are attractive plants when well grown, producing healthy clumps of attractively coloured flowers on short stems. They are indigenous to the Far East, with some of the best forms growing close to the Himalayan snow line. Perhaps a good plant for the orchid beginner to take an interest in.

GENERAL CARE These may be grown in a greenhouse designed for alpine plants, or in the cool section of an orchid house should one be available. It is not impossible to grow pleiones in pots on an outside windowsill.

PROPAGATION From small pseudobulbs removed from the parent.

VARIETIES The species is most frequently offered for sale, but there are varieties including 'Oriental splendour' (*above*).

POSSIBLE PROBLEMS Slugs and snails.

VANDA

| 1.2m/4ft | 60cm/24in | good light essential | 18°C/65°F | high |

Natives of South-east Asia and the Far East, vandas flower profusely over the winter months; they are capable of producing several flushes of flowers over one winter season. Flower colouring is very varied, with blue forms being especially choice.

GENERAL CARE Grow close to the window – if in a greenhouse suspend in a lath basket close to the glass and allow the roots to hang free. Water and allow to dry before repeating, but avoid long periods of drought. Feed fortnightly with balanced fertilizer. Provide a moisture-laden atmosphere, fresh air and bright light.

PROPAGATION From offsets removed from the parent plant when a few centimetres in length. Keep in moist, enclosed conditions until rooted.

SPECIES *Vanda coerulea*, *V. sanderana* and *V. rothschildiana*. Varieties include 'Rose Davis'.

POSSIBLE PROBLEMS Generally trouble-free.

▪ PLANTING TIP

To get the best from these plants they should be potted into fresh potting mixture in shallow pans each year prior to flowering. Plants are deciduous, the single pseudobulb lasting only one year. The bulb will produce 2 offsets and these can be removed for potting into fresh mixture, planted several to a pan of 12.5cm/5 in in diameter.

▪ CARE TIP

Vandas are plants that will often be seen growing in lath hanging baskets that seem absurdly small compared to the size of the plant; nevertheless, they will thrive like this if humidity, watering and feeding are attended to.

BONSAI

In the Far East the method of growing plants known as bonsai has been something of an art form for countless centuries, but 'indoor bonsai' seems to have crept into being with the advent of house plants. However, the many plants labelled 'temperate' or 'sub tropic' that are used for this purpose in the western world are run-of-the-mill materials in the tropics, suggesting that 'indoor bonsai' is not substantially different from the ancient art form. 'Indoor bonsai' has certainly raised the possibility of growing a very different range of plants within the home.

PURCHASING

The growing of indoor bonsai is one thing, but the first thought must be the acquisition of plant material that you can employ for bonsai purposes. Should you own some woodland, you can go out and dig up a few seedlings for the purpose of getting started with bonsai. Alernatively, there are specialist nurseries where more established plants may be acquired. However, for the average person seeking to experiment in a modest way with indoor bonsai the best source of material might well be your garden centre where, in the house plant department, you will find a wide range of plants that can be adopted for indoor bonsai culture.

LOCATION

Whether you intend to grow them as indoor bonsai or as conventional house plants, the location within the home for the assortment of plants you have chosen will

A bonsai grown juniper shows the pleasing tree shape characteristic of this art.

be relatively the same. House plants will generally have attached to them a care card with information concerning light, shade, temperature and such like, and a plant of, say, *Ficus benjamina* will require the same sort of location regardless of what your intentions in respect of culture may be. For the vast majority of plants for the home, the most important requirement is good light with some protection from strong sunlight. Generally speaking, plants with variegated or very colourful foliage require lighter locations than those with entirely green foliage.

CONDITIONS

Offering specific advice on this aspect of indoor bonsai culture is something of a problem as the chosen plants will be so varied in their temperature requirements. Temperate plants might well grow happily in the garden (to die in a severe winter!) or they may be of more delicate nature and need some cosseting to prosper. When buying you should get reliable advice concerning the needs of each particular purchase. Many of the less tender plants will normally do better if they can enjoy a sheltered and shaded spot out of doors for the summer months.

WATERING

Conventional plants in pots frequently become much too wet on account of the large volume of soil that is around their roots, and very wet conditions is one sure way of killing off container plants, regardless of the type of container. With indoor bonsai the containers are extremely shallow in many instances, with the result that there is very much less soil around the roots of the plant. A further advantage here is that the roots are very much better aerated, so providing ample oxygen for their well-being and, in turn, the well-being of the plant. But, with very little soil to retain moisture, it is important that indoor bonsai plants are checked very frequently for moisture requirements.

FEEDING

The need to keep indoor bonsai compact with frequent top and root pruning does not mean that nourishing the plant should be neglected – failing to feed the plant during its active season of growth will simply result in the yellowing and eventual loss of leaves. As time goes by you will become more knowledgeable about your plants' feeding requirements by means of experiment. Initially, however, it is advisable to use a balanced fertilizer that has been prepared for potted plants. The fertilizer can be a foliar feed, and there is the choice of high potash or high nitrogen preparations. The beginner might well decide that a tomato fertilizer is the most convenient and the most satisfactory. Only feed plants that are in active growth, so little or no feed is needed in winter.

POTTING AND POTTING MIXTURES

For the first steps in potting indoor bonsai plants it is advisable to avoid attempts at preparing soil concoctions that might be some way off the mark in terms of suitability. The best advice is to buy a ready-made bonsai potting mixture, which will have all the ingredients that the plant is likely to need. The time for potting the majority of plants will be January, but this can vary a little either way. Potting on is not the correct term for this exercise, as the majority of plants will be removed from their pots/containers to be replanted in the same container following any root pruning that may be found necessary.

TOOLS

The growing popularitiy of indoor bonsai means that there is a wide range of tools and general aids on sale that simplify the many tasks that will require attention. A good garden centre or a specialist supplier will be able to provide all that is needed.

PESTS AND DISEASES

Indoor bonsai will be affected by the same pests as any other indoor plants – vigilance is the answer, prevention being better than cure!

BOUGAINVILLEA

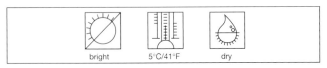

bright | 5°C/41°F | dry

Bougainvillea (paper flower) is a true tropical exotic that will shed most, or all, of its leaves in winter. In nature plants will develop very strong trunks with age, and for bonsai purposes the aim should be to have a central stem of some substance. This may well be possible in the early stages by selecting a stout branch for propagating. Growth from such a branch can then be trained to shape by selecting only a few of the most promising growths. With normal cultivation plants will produce their bract flowers from early March.

GENERAL CARE Provide a cool, light and airy location and never overwater, particularly in winter.

PROPAGATION Taken in February and given bottom heat of around 25°C/76°F, a leafless stem section of some 15cm/6 in length can be rooted without too much difficulty.

VARIETIES There are many to choose from in colours from white through orange to the deepest red.

POSSIBLE PROBLEMS Scale insects, aphids among others; excessive wet causes root failure.

BUXUS

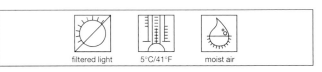

filtered light | 5°C/41°F | moist air

The common box, *Buxus sempervirens*, could well be used for experimental purposes during the initial steps with indoor bonsai. However, there are more tender Asiatic species, such as *B. harlandii*, that will be a touch more exotic – the temperature above refers to this type of plant, which is not winter-hardy.

GENERAL CARE Plants should be watered by immersing the pot until all the air-bubbles have escaped – the exercise to be repeated only when the soil has dried out. Feed established plants at fortnightly intervals while in active growth. Offer a lightly shaded location in cool conditions.

PROPAGATION By top cuttings in late summer, by layering or by dividing older plants. Cuttings are slow to mature.

VARIETIES As mentioned above, but also any other varieties of interest that may be obtainable.

POSSIBLE PROBLEMS Red spider mites cause leaf discoloration and general debility; aphids on young growth.

■ CARE TIP

In much of its native habitat bougainvillea is obliged to tolerate spartan conditions, which makes it a suitable subject for bonsai purposes. Bright conditions are important.

■ CARE TIP

When establishing young plants it is important not to allow the development of too much clumpy growth as this leads to a very unattractive plant. It is much better to thin out the weaker shoots and to aim at providing an attractive shape by selecting suitable stronger branches and training them into shape by using bonsai training wire. As with all bonsai, the establishment of a specimen tree is a long and slow process.

CAMELLIA

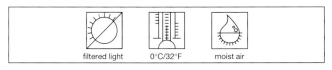

filtered light | 0°C/32°F | moist air

Native to the countries of the Far East, these are glossy-leaved, spring-flowering plants that must have frost protection for the blooms. For bonsai purposes a single stem that is trained to lean or is given a twist by careful wiring gives the plant a little more interest.

GENERAL CARE Ericaceous potting mixture, soft water and feeding with an ericaceous fertilizer are important needs of these decorative plants. Repotting is only needed every 2-3 years, and one should not be too severe when it comes to root pruning.

PROPAGATION From top cuttings taken in October and placed in fresh, moist peat with bottom heat in a greenhouse, or by layering.

VARIETIES Countless varieties, with the long-established C. 'Donation' still being one of the front runners.

POSSIBLE PROBLEMS Chlorotic conditions from using the wrong type of soil.

CITRUS

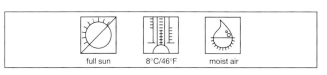

full sun | 8°C/46°F | moist air

The general name of citrus covers a number of exotic fruits,, many of which are too large to contemplate as bonsai for the average household. Choose one of the less robust varieties such as *Citrus mitis*, the calomondin orange, which can be had as a pleasing variegated form. The bonus here is that it also produces lots of small, edible oranges when growing well.

GENERAL CARE Root pruning at potting time must be done with care as these are not particularly strong-rooting plants. With judicious pruning of surplus shoots C. *mitis* will adopt a reasonably natural bonsai shape of its own accord.

PROPAGATION From firm top cuttings taken in the spring and rooted in bottom heat in a greenhouse. Results of seed propagation are unpredictable.

VARIETIES Numerous varieties are available from specialist growers, but one must stipulate compact or slow growth habit. Suitable plants are invariably in short supply.

POSSIBLE PROBLEMS Most troublesome are scale insects and red spider mites – take action as soon as detected.

▪ GENERAL TIP

It would be foolish to suggest that camellias would be at home if kept indoors throughout the year, as they really are outdoor plants. But they are also excellent plants for a window that is cool and light, or for decorating the conservatory while they are in flower. For most of the year they should enjoy a cool location out of doors.

▪ CARE TIP

The effects of scale insect attack on citrus plants can be especially displeasing as they leave an unattractive sooty deposit on the leaves – wipe clean with soapy water.

CRASSULA

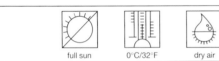

full sun   0°C/32°F   dry air

The best of these is *Crassula argentea* 'Sunset', with three-colour variegated leaves and a splendid pale brown stem. Mature container-grown plants have a distinctly bonsai look without need for bonsai treatment, but removal of the lower branches to expose the attractive stem and the stopping back of longer branches will much enhance the bonsai appearance.

GENERAL CARE To do well offer cool and light conditions and never overwater. Feed occasionally during the summer months. Plants that have spent the summer out of doors should be brought in as winter approaches, but never into very warm conditions. Plants will tolerate a touch of frost if the soil is very dry.

PROPAGATION Top cuttings allowed to dry before inserting in any reasonable soil in modest warmth will not prove difficult to root.

VARIETIES *C. argentea* 'Sunset', *C. argentea* (green foliage) and *C. arborescens* – a much bolder plant.

POSSIBLE PROBLEMS Generally trouble-free.

FICUS BENJAMINA

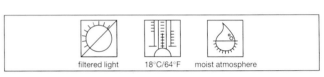

filtered light   18°C/64°F   moist atmosphere

Ficus benjamina (weeping fig) has naturally glossy leaves attached to elegant weeping branches; there are numerous close relatives. Bright green leaves against whitish stems set off this plant to perfection. It is an ideal subject for the beginner to indoor bonsai to experiment with, as it will not be difficult to train branches to provide interesting shapes. For a start young plants can be grown upright in their initial pots then potted on their sides to grow at an angle when introduced to their bonsai container.

GENERAL CARE Good light is essential for this plant, as are moist roots and regular feeding.

PROPAGATION From firm top or leaf cuttings taken at any time of the year provided bed temperature of 21°C/75°F can be maintained.

VARIETIES *F.b.* 'Golden Princess', *F.b.* 'Starlight', *F.b.* 'Hawaii' – all have variegated foliage.

POSSIBLE PROBLEMS Scale insects can be a problem; loss of leaves in poor light.

▪ GENERAL TIP

The variegated form of this plant, C.a. 'Sunset', could be an interesting plant for the beginner with indoor bonsai as the cuttings root very readily, giving the opportunity of conducting a few experiments. Grow plants as single stems by removing side shoots as they appear until such time as a stem of reasonable size develops, then experiment with shaping.

▪ GENERAL TIP

The natural weeping of the plant stems could be further exaggerated by attaching light weights to the stems to induce them to hang more interestingly. Avoid heavy weights as these might break branches.

JACARANDA

filtered light   15°C/50°F   moist atmosphere

With its full complement of amazing flowers this is a queen among tropical trees, but it is unlikely that flowers will be a feature when plants are being treated as indoor bonsai – for the later exercise the delicate foliage will be the main attraction. The best start will be to raise seed in a heated propagator and to plant a group of seedlings in a shallow dish filled with a loam-based free-draining potting mixture. When stems are still supple they can be wired into position to create a more pleasing effect.

GENERAL CARE These are plants that will do better in a light, sheltered location out of doors during the summer.

PROPAGATION From seed sown in moist conditions in a heated propagator.

SPECIES *Jacaranda mimosaefolia, J. obtusifolia.*

POSSIBLE PROBLEMS Aphids, scale insects and red spider mites.

MYRTUS

bright light   5°C/41°F   moist atmosphere

The flowers of myrtle are fragrant, as are the leaves when crushed, and the plant has a pleasing, fresh green appearance. These are fine plants for container growing, as bonsai or otherwise. Plants should be trained to shape in the spring by removing much of the inner growth to reduce the dense, clumpy appearance. At this time, too, the stouter branches that remain can be wired to the desired shape.

GENERAL CARE Provide cool, light and airy conditions for best results. Avoid late pruning of branches as this will result in many fewer flowers later in the season. During the spring and summer months plants will benefit from a sheltered outdoor location.

PROPAGATION From cuttings in early summer using a sandy mixture and a heated propagator.

SPECIES *Myrtus bullata* (common myrtle); *M.b.* 'Variegata', white variegation on leaves; *M. microphylla*, smaller leaves; *M. torentina*, more compact.

POSSIBLE PROBLEMS Aphids, red spider mites, among others.

▇ DESIGN TIP

When preparing plants with feathery, delicate foliage for indoor bonsai it is advisable to plant them in groups rather than as individuals. This will mean obtaining a shallow dish of reasonably large dimension so that the plants can be arranged to maximum effect and the need for too much disturbance at an early date will be limited.

▇ PLANTING TIP

When potting plants such as the myrtle that will spend long periods of time out of doors it is wise to cover the holes in the bottom of the container with perforated zinc to deter worms.

PODOCARPUS

filtered sun	5°C/41°F	moist air

Podocarpus are tropical forest trees found from Africa to New Zealand. If there is a choice select those with narrow, yew-like foliage as they are more decorative as bonsai. With evergreen leaves it can become a substantial plant even when confined to a container. These are plants that can be wire-trained into interesting shapes with a true miniaturized forest look about them.

GENERAL CARE Protection from frost is necessary, but plants can remain outside for much of the year if desired. Keep moist and feed fortnightly while in active growth, giving less water and no feed over winter. Mist foliage during summer in a dry room atmosphere.

PROPAGATION From cuttings in a heated propagator or from seed.

VARIETIES *Podocarpus elongatus*, *P. macrophyllus* (Buddhist pine), and *P.m.* 'Maki', with larger, attractive glossy leaves.

POSSIBLE PROBLEMS Red spider mites, scale insects among others.

POLYSCIAS

filtered sun	8°C/46°F	moist atmosphere

The polyscias (dinner-plate aralias) are tropical relatives of the ivy and when container-grown are painfully slow movers – an advantage in respect of indoor bonsai, as many of the numerous varieties have a bonsai appearance even when grown naturally. Grouping several plants in a flat dish is one way of setting plants off to advantage; the variety *Polyscias fruticosa* has finely segmented foliage that is well suited to this style of planting.

GENERAL CARE Keep moist and fed fortnightly when in active growth, with no feeding in winter and less generous watering. Although related to the ivy these are more temperamental plants, needing careful winter attention.

PROPAGATION From cuttings, or root cuttings taken in the spring and placed in a heated propagator.

SPECIES *P. balfouriana* and its several cultivars and *P. fruticosa* are the most readily available.

POSSIBLE PROBLEMS Red spider mites and scale insects; root loss from cold and wet winter conditions.

■ PLANTING TIP

The podocarpus belongs to the family Podocarpaceae, but has a pine-like appearance when grown as bonsai. Like the pine, it is a substantial plant when grown in a container. For this reason one should ensure that the chosen container is reasonably substantial and that there are 2 holes in the bottom through which wires can be drawn to anchor the plant.

■ DESIGN TIP

The stems of the polyscias will become bare lower down as they age – in many ways an attraction, but appearance will be improved if interesting stones can be incorporated in the design.

PUNICA GRANATUM

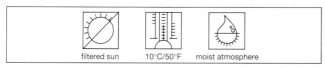

filtered sun | 10°C/50°F | moist atmosphere

Of the numerous pomegranates, the plant most often offered for sale is *Punica granatum* 'Nana', the dwarf pomegranate. When container-grown, plants will produce their orange to red flowers but the fruits that develop are generally very small with a tendency to split. For indoor bonsai purposes these provide neat plants with a stout central stem once they have become established. The branches should be thinned out to provide a somewhat sparse effect, with wiring to shape done when the branches are firm but still pliable.

GENERAL CARE Keep soil moist and feed fortnightly during the growing season, with very much less water and no feeding at other times. The leaves are shed in winter; do necessary repotting prior to the appearance of new leaves.

PROPAGATION By seed, if obtainable, in the spring, or firm cuttings in mid summer – both done in peat and sand in a heated propagator.

VARIETIES *P.g.* 'Florepleno', 'Legrellei', and 'Nana'.

POSSIBLE PROBLEMS Aphids, red spider mites; chlorotic yellowing of leaves in poor growing conditions.

SAGERETIA THEEZANS

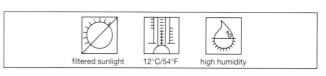

filtered sunlight | 12°C/54°F | high humidity

This is a tender tree needing warm conditions to survive. The glossy evergreen leaves are an attraction in themselves, added to which the tree has attractive bark that is not unlike that of a mature plane tree.

GENERAL CARE Indoors, plants must be kept moist at all times with rather less water given in winter. A humid environment is also important and entails the need for periodic misting around the plant. Pruning can be undertaken at any time of the year; any repotting should be done in the spring every second or third year.

PROPAGATION Firm young cuttings should be taken in the spring and placed in a heated propagating case.

VARIETIES The above is the only plant that may be obtainable.

POSSIBLE PROBLEMS Aphids, red spider mites; chlorotic foliage from indifferent culture.

▦ CARE TIP

In milder regions pomegranates can be planted out of doors against a sheltered wall, but it is preferable to grow them either indoors or in a greenhouse. A combination of spending part of the year in the greenhouse (winter), part indoors (spring) and part in a sheltered location outside (summer) is best of all.

▦ CARE TIP

Root prune indoor bonsai when plants are pot-bound. Remove the plant from its container, disentangle the roots and, with sharp secateurs, trim off one-third of the roots. Repot in the same container with fresh soil.

GLOSSARY

Acid Used to describe soil with a pH reading below 7.0. Because acid soils contain little lime, lime-hating plants like azaleas thrive.

Active growth The period during the annual cycle when a plant produces new leaves and flowers and increases in size.

Aerial roots Roots arising from stems above the growing medium, e.g. some orchids.

Alkaline Used to describe soil with a pH reading above 7.0. A slightly alkaline soil suits most plants.

Axil The angle between the stem and a leaf, from which further growth arises.

Bract A modified leaf, which may be brightly coloured and have the appearance of a petal, e.g. bromeliads, *Euphorbia pulcherrima*.

Bulb An underground storage organ made up of tightly wrapped fleshy leaves or leaf bases.

Bulbil A small bulb that forms at the base of mature bulbs which can be detached and grown on to achieve maturity.

Chlorosis Deficiency of minerals in the growing medium giving a pale appearance to foliage.

Compost A mixture of loam, sand, peat and leaf-mould used for growing plants in containers.

Corm An underground storage organ formed by a thickened leaf base. Unlike a bulb, a corm does not contain the young plant.

Crown The basal part of a plant from which roots and shoots arise.

Cutting A portion of a plant removed and used to raise a new plant; usually from a stem or leaf.

Dead-heading Removing faded flower-heads in order to encourage further flowering and keep a plant looking attractive.

Dormant Literally, sleeping. Used to describe the period when a plant makes no growth, usually in the winter.

Epiphytic Used to describe plants which can live without having their roots in soil, e.g. many bromeliads and orchids.

Forcing Bringing plants into flower before their natural time.

Frond The leaf of a palm or fern.

Fungicide A substance used to combat fungal diseases.

Germination The first stage in the development of a plant from a seed.

Hardy Description of plants that survive frost in the open.

Heel The base of a piece of stem which has been torn away from a side shoot to be used as a cutting. Cuttings often root more readily if a heel is attached.

Hybrid A plant that results from the crossing of two species or varieties, e.g. × *Fatshedera lizei*.

Insecticide A substance used for killing insects.

Lateral A stem or shoot that branches out from the leaf axil of a larger stem.

Leader The main stem of a plant.

Lime Calcium, a chemical that may be used to neutralize acid soils. Too much lime makes it impossible for certain nutrients in the growing medium to be absorbed by plants.

Loam Soil which is a compound of clay, silt, sand and humus. It is an ingredient of soil-based composts and is always sterilized for commercial use to purify it of harmful organisms.

Node A joint in a plant's stem from which leaves, buds and side-shoots arise.

Offset A young plant that is naturally produced by mature (or 'parent') plants and can be detached and used for propagation.

Peat Partially decayed organic matter. An important ingredient of proprietary composts and used in combination with sand to raise cuttings.

Pendent Literally, hanging. Used to describe flowers like those of the fuchsia.

Perennial A plant that lives for an indefinite period.

pH reading The pH scale is used to measure the acidity or alkalinity of soil. The neutral point is 7.0; a reading above this denotes alkalinity and one below it denotes acidity.

Pinching out Removing the growing point of a stem to encourage bushy growth.

Potbound Used to describe a plant whose roots have completely filled the pot and can no longer efficiently support it; an indication that repotting is necessary.

Pricking out Planting out seedlings for the first time to larger trays or individual pots.

Propagation Increasing or raising new plants, either from seed or vegetatively, i.e. from cuttings, offsets or suckers.

Pruning Cutting back a plant to keep the shape neat and restrict the size.

Repotting Transferring a plant which has outgrown its pot and exhausted the nutrients in its compost to a larger pot containing fresh compost.

Rhizome An underground storage organ composed of a creeping stem.

Rootball Used to describe a plant's roots and the growing medium supporting them.

Rosette An arrangement of leaves radiating from a central point.

Spadix A flower spike containing numerous tiny flowers.

Spathe A large bract enclosing a spadix e.g. *Spathiphyllum* 'Mauna Loa'.

Spore A minute particle by which ferns reproduce themselves.

Stake A support for a plant.

Stolon A creeping stem which roots at the nodes where they make contact with the growing medium e.g. *Saxifraga stolonifera*.

Succulent A plant with fleshy leaves or stems which can store water and survive arid conditions.

Sucker A shoot that arises below the level of the growing medium and which in some species can be used for propagation.

Tender Used to describe any plant susceptible to damage by frost.

Terrestrial Growing in the soil.

Topdress Applying fresh compost to a plant after first removing 2.5-5 cm/1-2 inches of the old compost. Useful for sustaining mature plants which have reached the largest convenient pot size.

Tuber An underground storage organ, either a thickened root or stem.

Variegated Used to describe leaves which are marked with a contrasting colour.

INDEX